Working in the Reggio Way

A Beginner's Guide for American Teachers

Working in the Reggio Way

A Beginner's Guide for American Teachers

JULIANNE WURM

Redleaf Press
St. Paul, Minnesota
www.redleafpress.org

naeyc

Published by Redleaf Press
a division of Resources for Child Caring
10 Yorkton Court
St. Paul, MN 55117
Visit us online at www.redleafpress.org

National Association for the
Education of Young Children
1509 16th Street NW
Washington, DC 20036

Cover design by Brad Norr Design
Interior design by Brian Donohue, Be Design
Typography and composition by Dorie McClelland, Spring Book Design

The views expressed in this publication are those of the author, representing her own interpretation of the philosophy and practices of the Municipal Infant-Toddler Centers and Preschools of Reggio Emilia. The content of this publication has not been officially approved by the Municipality of Reggio Emilia or by Reggio Children in Italy; therefore it may not reflect the views and opinions of these organizations. Reggio Children, Via Bligny 1, 42100 Reggio Emilia, Italy, tel: +39 0522 513752, http://zerosei.comune.re.it/inter/reggiochildren.htm

Redleaf Press books are available at a special discount when purchased in bulk for special premiums and sales promotions. For details, contact the sales manager at 800-423-8309.

Library of Congress Cataloging-in-Publication Data
Wurm, Julianne, 1969–
 Working in the Reggio way : a beginner's guide for American teachers / Julianne Wurm.
  p. cm.
 ISBN-10: 1-929610-64-5 (pbk.)
 ISBN-13: 978-1-929610-64-8
 1. Education, Preschool—Italy—Reggio Emilia. 2. Early childhood education—Italy—Reggio Emilia. 3. School management and organization—Italy—Reggio Emilia. I. Title.
 LB1140.25.18W87 2005
 372.21—dc22
                              2005004207

Manufactured in the United States of America
12 11 10 09 08 07 06 05   1 2 3 4 5 6 7 8

TO MY GRANDMOTHER, LOIS WURM,
WITH ENDURING GRATITUDE FOR ALL SHE MODELED ABOUT BEING HUMAN

Contents

CHAPTER 5: Observation and Documentation 97

CHAPTER 6: Families 123

No way. The hundred is there.

BY LORIS MALAGUZZI

The child
is made of one hundred.
The child has
a hundred languages
a hundred hands
a hundred thoughts
a hundred ways of thinking
of playing, of speaking.
A hundred always a hundred
ways of listening
of marveling of loving
a hundred joys
for singing and understanding
a hundred worlds
to discover
a hundred worlds
to invent
a hundred worlds
to dream.
The child has
a hundred languages
(and a hundred hundred hundred more)
but they steal ninety-nine.
The school and the culture
separate the head from the body.
They tell the child:
to think without hands

to do without head
to listen and not to speak
to understand without joy
to love and to marvel
only at Easter and at Christmas.
They tell the child:
to discover the world already there
and of the hundred
they steal ninety-nine.
They tell the child:
that work and play
reality and fantasy
science and imagination
sky and earth
reason and dream
are things
that do not belong together.

And thus they tell the child
that the hundred is not there.
The child says:
No way. The hundred is there.

"No way. The hundred is there." by Loris Malaguzzi from *The Hundred Languages of Children Exhibit Catalogue*, © Infant-Toddler Centers and Preschools—Instituzione of the Municipality of Reggio Emilia, published by Reggio Children, 1996. Translated by Lella Gandini. Reprinted with permission from Reggio Children.

Taking an educational approach like that identified with Reggio Emilia, Italy, out of its cultural context can be daunting. Yet in these pages Julianne Wurm accepts the challenge while also accepting the unique aspects of a widely known early childhood setting. Note that I have not used the word *program* to refer to Reggio Emilia, for it is not a step-by-step program to be followed like a script. Instead it is a philosophy that encompasses the nature of children, learning, and teaching—a philosophy that can be enacted by those who understand the philosophy by experiencing it day by day, over time.

You will find in these pages an accessible and engaging invitation to learn about your ways of learning and teaching at the same time that you are learning how children and teachers enact Reggio ways. Because Julie has herself experienced Reggio ways in Reggio classrooms, she can raise questions for us that she herself struggled to answer. For example, What does the arrangement of furniture and equipment in our rooms tell us about our view of children? How do active teachers fit close observation into their days? How can we use still photographs to capture the always-moving learning process? These are not brand-new questions, but the answers to them are going to be unique. They will be constructed by us, the readers, as Julie guides our own construction and understanding of Reggio ways.

My experience in classrooms in the city of Reggio Emilia has been brief, remarkably positive, and memorable. Despite the briefness, Julie's detailed descriptions of classrooms in which she worked alongside children and their teachers and families ring true. The mutual respect among these groups—children, teachers, families—becomes palpable, as we read and picture ourselves alongside them. In the current educational world in the United States, many of us are increasingly faced with scripted curricula that require little knowledge of children's learning and even less imagination. We need books like Julie's to help ourselves imagine changes, no matter how small, in classrooms where children and adults enjoy the space and time to construct their own ways of learning and teaching.

Celia Genishi
Teachers College, Columbia University

Acknowledgments

With special thanks to the following:

My enduring thanks for the encouragement, patience, and intellect of my editor, Beth Wallace.

Love and thanks to my father, James Wurm, for always reserving your judgment and supporting me as I crept along on my path. I have always known you were on my side when others dismissed my ideas as impossible.

Professionally, I am deeply grateful to and enriched by my colleagues in Reggio Emilia who have so generously shared their knowledge—Paola Ascari, Patrizia Margini, Antonia Ferrari, GianCarla Beltrami, Mara Davoli, Gino Ferri, Lucia Colla, Barbara Fabbi, Simonetta Bottacini, Roberta Moscatelli, Tiziana Filipini. Many thanks as well to my friends in Reggio—Margherita Sani, Carolina Foglia, Giovanni Foglia and Claudio Foglia, Maurillio Sordi and Antonio Nocco, Corrado Cassone, Gian Luigi Pascarella, Manuela Calderini, Leslie Morrow, Jackie Costa, Sandra Bernardi, Patrizio Zaccarelli, Ivana and Luca Guidetti and Alberto Cantarelli—for making my life in Reggio rich. Many American colleagues have provided me continued opportunities for personal and professional growth. Many thanks to Tom Drummond, Celia Genishi, Sam Shreyar, Davida Desmond, Michele Anberg-Espinosa, Kristin Carver, Mark Alvarado, Hydra Mendoza, Danny Guillory, Karling Aguilera-Fort, Adelina Aramburo, Joan Hepperly, Linda Luevano, and Jeanne Villafuerte. I offer my thanks to each of the people who have listened to me and encouraged me personally—Amy and Brad Davis, Dr. Jonathan Shifren, Sandy and Gaven Dunn, Amy and Rob Liss, Tim and Heather Swan, Bill and Karin Davis, Doug and Diane Cooper, Heidi and Sean Castagna, Wendy and Dan DaDalt, Nancy and Eric Windeshiem-Zigas, Angela Basile, Sean O'Byrne, Stacy Douglas, Jori Steck, and Marc Seitles. Without all of your contributions I would never have done this project.

To one of the human beings I like the most, Vidal Perez—thank you, truly.

Most important, many thanks to all of the children I have had the privilege to work with, who have taught me so much.

If your mind is still open enough to question what you are seeing, you tend to look at the world with great care, and out of that watchfulness comes the possibility of seeing something that no one else has seen before. You have to be willing to admit that you don't have all the answers. If you think you do, you will never have anything important to say.

—PAUL AUSTER, *True Tales of American Life*

Introduction

The municipal early childhood programs of Reggio Emilia, Italy, have created an educational reality that many other educators strive to achieve. A 1991 *Newsweek* article identified the programs in Reggio Emilia as the best early childhood programs in the world ("The Ten Best Schools in the World, and What We Can Learn from Them," December 2, 1991) and thrust them into the international spotlight. Since then, a series of publications, study tours, exhibits, and conferences have fueled the interest and marvel surrounding these programs. They are widely recognized as the best early childhood has to offer, and remain a focal point of discussion and work in American early childhood education.

The Reggio schools began modestly after World War II, when the Italian government gave each *provincia,* or town, a small amount of money to use as they pleased to help restore the sense of community lost during the war. Most towns built community centers to offer a place for the people to gather. However, in Villa Cella, slightly outside the center of Reggio Emilia, the inhabitants decided to build a school for the children as an investment in the future: *Scuola del popolo,* School of the People.

Once decided, the determined Italians began working. During the week the women would gather bricks from bombed out buildings, and on the weekends the men would build. They named the first school *Scuola XXV Aprile,* or April 25th School, after the day of liberation from the Nazis. Loris Malaguzzi, who is known as the father of the Reggio approach to education, heard about this project in Villa Cella and thought it impossible. He got on his bicycle and rode out to see if it was true. When he arrived, he discovered that in fact the rumors were true and the citizens were building a school literally brick by brick. He is said to have decided to become a part of this project because it changed the definition of the word *impossible.* Loris Malaguzzi went on to become the driving force behind the approach to education embodied in the Reggio schools, which has developed over the fifty years since the first school opened.

As a testament to and an example of the work done in Reggio Emilia, a traveling exhibit titled "The Hundred Languages of Children" made its first appearance in 1980 and its first trip to North America in

1987. Since the exhibit began touring and the *Newsweek* article further publicized the Reggio approach to early childhood education, thousands of educators from around the world have visited the Municipal Preschools of Reggio Emilia, Italy. The classic text introducing North Americans to the Reggio approach, *The Hundred Languages of Children: The Reggio Emilia Approach* (edited by Carolyn Edwards, Lella Gandini, and George Forman), was first published in 1993 and is now in its second edition.

Reggio Children, a separate entity from the preschools, was established in 1994 with the mission "to manage the pedagogical and cultural exchange initiatives that had already been taking place for many years between the municipal early childhood services and a large number of teachers and researchers from all over the world" (from the Web site of Reggio Children: http://zerosei.comune.re.it/inter/reggiochildren.htm). The exhibit, publications, and study tours have encouraged educators to embrace the Reggio approach, and schools around the world are now working in Reggio-inspired ways, adapting the approach of the Reggio schools to their own cultural settings. Every year groups from Europe, South America, the United States, Canada, Australia, and New Zealand tour the Reggio schools.

My Experience in Reggio Emilia

My journey to Reggio Emilia began quite by accident in 1997, when I visited Italy one summer on vacation from a master's program at Columbia Teachers College. While in Italy, I heard about some famous Italian preschools from Italian friends. When I returned to New York, I asked my professors and colleagues about these schools. Then I did an ERIC search (ERIC is a database of abstracts of journal articles and other documents related to education), but all of the articles I found were not as specific as I wanted. It was difficult to find a first-person account that spoke clearly about this educational approach. To become informed about Reggio Emilia, I decided I needed to go to Italy and see these schools. I needed to work inside them, in *prima persona,* the first person. I finished the degree I was working on, sold my belongings, and moved to Europe.

I moved to the town of Reggio Emilia in 1998 and spent a year learning Italian and working as a teacher of English. In July 1999 I was granted permission to work in the preschools as a full-time intern for the 1999–2000 school year. I started the internship without having read the best-known American book about Reggio, *The Hundred Languages of Children.* I decided to go in without any preconceived idea of what I would find. I wanted to see what I could learn without already knowing too much. I could fill in the theoretical gaps after I had the first-person practical experience. I was interested in seeing what actually happened, how the teachers really worked. So, when I arrived at the doors of the Scuola dell'Infanzia Pablo Neruda on September 19, 1999, and began working alongside the teachers, I had much less information than most teachers who visit Reggio. I was amazed: I now understood why teachers came to Reggio Emilia for the opportunity to pass, however briefly, through these schools.

I spent September and October in Scuola Pablo Neruda with the four-year-olds and their teachers, Patty and Paola. In November I went to the fives with Lara and Antonia. In January 2000 I went to the threes, with Simonetta, Roberta, and Delia. Towards the end of February, it was left up to me to follow projects and children who were the most interesting. Teachers also began to invite me into their rooms to work on projects. In the spring of 2000 it was arranged for me to go and spend a couple of months at Nido Bellelli to see the program for children under three. In early May I returned to Neruda, my home school, until the first week of July, when summer vacation began.

While in Reggio I also worked as an interpreter for international delegations, enabling me to speak to hundreds of teachers from around the world who participated in the study tours of Reggio. Each delegation had its own unique identity, as teachers from each country came with a bit of their own culture. This was helpful in looking at the practices inside the schools of Reggio Emilia too. It was like putting on different-colored glasses and looking at the same thing. Different elements were highlighted while others faded to the background, depending on the cultural perspective.

Barriers to Taking Reggio Home

Many visitors were enthusiastic when they arrived in Reggio and began touring the preschools. There is the sense of well-being when entering a place that is so well cared for and aesthetically pleasing, and that functions simply and so well. I saw over time, however, that many visitors became overwhelmed as the week progressed—as if the experience was daunting instead of inspiring.

My work as an interpreter for international delegations gave me the opportunity to eavesdrop on conversations between the Reggio teachers and their visitors from around the world. I realized there was a gap between the information that was sought and the information that was provided. It resulted from a mixture of things: language, different working situations, professional development experiences, and, most important, culture. Visitors to the schools were inspired about the possibilities they saw in Reggio, but many of them were confused about the first steps to move their programs in that direction.

Visitors asked many of the same questions that I had asked myself at the beginning of my internship. Their questions focused on organizational and logistical components, without examining the underlying reasons that the teachers in Reggio did things a certain way. While I had the opportunity over time to move past initial impressions and those organizational questions, the teachers touring the schools did not. Therefore, they were often left with impressions that only touched the surface of what went on in the preschools, and without the answers they sought. The fact that the schools are so impressive also presented visitors with some fears about the possibility of re-creating what they were seeing in their own schools. Many visitors brought up legal and financial limitations to creating something like the Reggio schools in their home countries. Many discussions also concerned the difficulty of motivating teachers to work in the very detailed and time-consuming ways seen in Reggio Emilia. Many visitors left their study tours having dismissed as an impossible goal the idea of creating a school like the Reggio schools.

When I returned to the United States in the summer of 2001, I began giving workshops and talking with teachers and directors around the country. Again, I found that many teachers who were interested in using the Reggio approach had trouble getting inside the Italian way of thinking. It is difficult for teachers in Reggio to break down the approach into smaller pieces because they see it all as interconnected—a big, complex picture. This is very different from the American mentality, which has a tendency to compartmentalize things and look at them individually, in small pieces. In addition, the teachers in Reggio are heirs to fifty years of work in what has become a well-established tradition. They are in a different place developmentally than the visitors pouring through their schools. Most of them were not present for the beginning of the Reggio schools, when what has become "the Reggio approach" was being developed and the same kinds of questions were being asked in Reggio.

Through my work with American schools and with teachers both in Italy and the United States, I saw that many American teachers who wanted to work in the Reggio way were challenged by similar problems: fluidity versus control, emergent versus prepared curriculum, knowing the answers versus questioning, and the Reggio approach to time, which is more relaxed and open-ended than most Americans are comfortable with. My experience in Reggio, together with my knowledge of early childhood and my teaching experience, put me in the unique position to articulate what I had seen and learned. My years in Reggio gave me the opportunity to watch, note, reflect, discuss, question, and re-question. From the perspective of an American in Reggio, I was able to investigate many questions that other teachers have posed but have not had the time or opportunity to explore in the same manner.

How to Use This Book

This book offers a tour of the Reggio approach through the eyes of a foreigner with one foot in both cultures. Unlike many other American books on the Reggio approach to early childhood education, this book is neither my personal story of applying Reggio principles in the United States nor a theoretical look at those principles. It is a practical guide to help reshape your thinking towards working with young children. It asks practical questions and suggests concrete activities that will help you answer those questions for yourself. The discussion and corresponding activities in the book are drawn directly from my experience as a participant-observer in the preschools of Reggio Emilia, Italy.

Starting to work with children in Reggio ways must begin with reflective practice—looking at the ways you are working and asking questions of yourself and your colleagues. This entails taking responsibility for your own professional development, which requires constant reflection, collaboration, and questioning. This book will help you take those first steps by giving you guidance in reflecting and questioning. I will ask you to start from the place where you are currently working and examine your own values about children, education, and community. We will look at some of the things I have seen in Reggio, and then we will try to build a bridge between your values and setting, and Reggio-inspired practice.

The book has been divided into chapters that compartmentalize the approach as much as possible. It is important to keep in mind that the separation is artificial—all elements of the approach are interconnected. It is also crucial to understand that there are no absolutes in the Reggio approach—no single answer or right way to do something. There are multiple ways of doing anything depending on the children and on the context. Even if I were to say, "In Reggio they do it like this ...," it would be the way it was done one time in one school by one group of teachers. It could never be considered the rule for everyone. I will use firsthand examples and anecdotes from the schools of Reggio, but these are not blueprints to be copied. What is done in Reggio Emilia cannot be copied with the hopes of creating an authentic educational experience for young children. Instead, you can start by asking questions and pushing your practice along the path that is Reggio-inspired.

I will ask you to begin with some simple yet significant questions concerning your view of the child and childhood, as well as questions about learning and education and the relationships that exist between these concepts.

Once you have had the opportunity to articulate your vision, I will take you through examining the environment in which you work. Is it reflective of your vision? Are your stated vision, your view of the child, and the environment aligned? This is the most difficult part of your work. Once you have articulated your view of the child and formulated your vision, everything in your school needs to reflect those values. Through the lens of your values about children and childhood, you will look at the physical environment and space; the organization of time; the Reggio approach to curriculum through *progettazione,* or projects; and then the documentation, questioning, and observation that give life to the curriculum and the program.

If you find that what you do or what exists in your school is not in keeping with your views and vision in one or more of these categories (and trust me, we all find that there are gaps between what we believe and what we do!), you have a couple of options. You can revise your vision, or you can change your program to reflect your vision. This is the real work this book will ask you to do. It will take time, and sometimes difficult and conflicting choices, but this process is the rigorous path towards working in Reggio-inspired ways, which is different for each school and teacher.

It is useful to have a notebook to accompany this book in which you can do the exercises, take notes for yourself, and record your responses to questions and how they evolve as the process progresses. You may want to form a group of teachers to work through the book together; you will learn much more and hone your collaboration skills if you work with other teachers.

Throughout the book, a number of Italian terms are used where English translations are inadequate to express the Italian concept. The following glossary was originally translated and compiled by Leslie Morrow, an interpreter with extensive experience working for the schools of Reggio. I have expanded and rewritten the glossary for the purposes of this book.

Glossary

Adulti: Reggio educators often use *adulti* when referring to teachers, both *atelieristas* and *pedagogistas*—the adults who work with the children. However, it can also include parents.

Atelier: The "studio" of the *atelierista*, where she or the teachers work with small groups of children; also used as a place for meetings, documentation, etc.

Atelierista: One for each preschool; a person with a background in the arts (most of the *nidi* have an *atelier* but not an *atelierista*). The *atelierista* helps teachers and children work with a variety of materials (media such as wire, clay, paint, computers) and is also integrally involved in the process of documentation.

Documentazione: documentation; this is an ongoing process, not simply the products and panels produced.

Mini-atelier: A separate space within or adjacent to each preschool classroom *(sezione)* having the same types of materials as the *atelier,* where small groups of children can work on particular projects with or without a teacher.

Nido: infant-toddler center (plural: *nidi*).

Pedagogista: Member of the *equipe pedagogica,* which is composed of eight people with degrees in education or psychology, each of whom coordinates a small group of four to five *nidi/scuole* and is the liaison between the schools and the administration (there are no "principals" or "head teachers" in the Reggio schools).

Progettazione: A way of working with children on projects or curriculum, but encompassing a larger way of thinking and working on the part of the staff, parents, administration, schools, etc. Often people have tried to define this using terms more familiar to them, such as *emergent curriculum, project approach,* or even *projected curriculum.* However, *progettazione* is more complex than any of these definitions.

Provocare: to provoke. However, as used in the Reggio program, a closer translation in English might be *to challenge* or *to stimulate.*

Provocazione: provocation. However, in English the meaning is closer to *stimulation* or *thought-provoker.*

Scuola dell'infanzia: preschool.

Sezione: (referring to groupings) For the *nido* this term refers to the group. Children in the *nidi* are grouped into four *sezioni:*

lattanti: infants
piccoli: toddlers 1
medi: toddlers 2
grandi: toddlers 3

Preschool classes are usually divided by age—threes, fours, and fives—though some schools have a fourth class, which is a mixed age group (the ages depend on the particular year).

Sezione: (referring to place) classroom.

The more time you spend with children, the more you notice how inquisitive they are about the world and how keen is their thinking even about the most subtle things—things which escape materiality, easy recognition, definite forms, and the laws of invariance, things you can touch but can't touch, that brush against the real and imaginary, that have something of the mysterious about them and offer wide margins of interpretation.

—LORIS MALAGUZZI

Chapter 1

Vision

The view we have of children is present in all that we do as educators. It can be seen in the way we present materials, the way we maintain our spaces, and even the food we serve. For example, do students eat reheated lunch on paper plates? What does this say about the view of the child as competent or valuable? What does it say about the value the program places on food or eating together or the sense of community? Is the bathroom door always closed, so children do not go without supervision? What does this say about the program's understanding of children as independent or, again, competent? Are materials creatively displayed at a child's level for easy access and inspection, or in a closed cabinet that only teachers are supposed to open? Each choice springs from a different understanding of the child's place in the classroom and the teacher's role.

In any educational project a vision underlies the work and is tied directly to your view of the child. Opinions about the place of children in society and the role that the education of children plays in their development are also influential. Carla Rinaldi, one of the best-known voices associated with Reggio Emilia, was a pedagogical coordinator or *pedagogista* in the Reggio Emilia programs. Eventually she became the director of Early Childhood Education in Reggio Emilia. Ms. Rinaldi is now the executive consultant to Reggio Children, the international institution devoted to research and the dissemination of the Reggio Emilia Approach to Early Childhood Education. In "The Thought That Sustains Educational Action" ("I pensieri che sostengono l'azione educativa") (Reggio Emilia, Italy: Reggio Children, 1994), she shares some fundamental questions that can begin to give shape to your view of the child and create a foundation for the vision upon which your school will function:

- Who is a child?
- What is childhood?
- How do we learn?
- How do children learn?
- What is the meaning of *to educate*?
- What is the relationship between teaching and learning?
- What is the relationship between theory and practice?
- What is the role of school in society?
- What is the relationship between school and research? And what is the relationship between schools for young children and research?
- What is the relationship between school and education?

Your first task in this book is to begin to answer these questions for yourself. Your answers to these questions will shape the work you do in the rest of this book and ultimately the work you do with children. Please keep in mind that this may take a significant amount of time and reflection on the experiences you have already had working with young children. Permit yourself the opportunity to explore these questions slowly and in depth, and be aware that your answers to them will change over time as you think about them more and more deeply. It is not a question of right and wrong answers, but of determining what you really believe about children and education, and then making sure that all the millions of decisions you make as you work with children reflect that vision to the best of your capacity. Give yourself permission to revisit and revise your answers as you work. Consider them works in progress. Continue reading this chapter with these questions in mind before trying to write anything down. It is important to always keep in mind that you are not trying to replicate what is believed in Reggio nor replicate the schools, as cultural restraints make that impossible. However, you can articulate what is true for you and culturally relevant in the United States.

On this note, it is worth examining the change in the United States of the view of children in the last twenty-five years. Recently the television show *60 Minutes* featured a program by correspondent Steve Kroft on Americans' changing view of children (October 3, 2004). The show discussed the "echo boomers," also known as "Generation Y" or the "millennials": a generation of Americans that spans from children now attending elementary school to young adults just out of college. According to historian Neil Howe, who has made a career of studying different generations, "They came along at a time when we started re-valuing kids. During the '60s and '70s, the frontier of reproductive medicine was contraception. During the '80s and beyond, it's been fertility and scouring the world to find orphan kids that we can adopt. . . . The culture looked down on kids. Now it wants kids; it celebrates them." (www.cbsnews.com/stories/2004/10/01/60 minutes/main646890.shtml). According to Howe, this group of children has been scheduled with classes and extra-curricular activities as never seen before in the United States.

One interesting finding of this research is that part of our society does not view the child as powerful, competent, and strong, but rather sees children as weak and in need of protection. "Parents feel as if they're holding onto a piece of Baccarat crystal or something that could somehow shatter at any point," says Dr. Mel Levine, who has studied the echo boomers at the University of North Carolina. "Parents really have a sense that their kids are fragile." According to Levine, children in this generation are not usually left to their own devices to pursue their imagination or interests. This phenomenon is part of the culture surrounding preschool programs in the United States. While this may not be your individual view, it is likely to be the view of at least some of the parents who bring their children to your school. As you think about this perception, you may discover ways that you also see children as fragile. This is the kind of cultural factor that must be considered when you think about how to adapt the Reggio approach to make it work in an American program.

Your View of the Child

In your journal, reflect on and record your responses to the following questions:

- Who is a child?
- What is childhood?
- How do we learn?
- How do children learn?
- What is the meaning of *to educate*?
- What is the relationship between teaching and learning?
- What is the relationship between theory and practice?
- What is the role of school in society?
- What is the relationship between school and research? And what is the relationship between schools for young children and research?
- What is the relationship between school and education?

Don't try to make your responses perfect. There really are no right or wrong answers to these questions. The journal should be an evolving record of your thinking, which will change as your practice changes. The form does not matter—you can use bullet points, a list of words, or short paragraphs. Simply begin responding to the best of your ability. Ideally, this continued exercise of stating and re-working your views will frame a great deal of the work that follows—not only your thinking about children, but what you translate from this book into your practice.

Remember that by examining and declaring your own values about children and education, as well as your view of the child, you are making a commitment to manifest these values in your work. In the projects you do, in the spaces you create, in the words you use with your students, when a decision must be made regarding your school in any capacity, it must be in keeping with your stated values, or the values must be revised.

Ideally, as you progress through the book and work through many of the other exercises, you will see where what you believe about children and what you are doing in your program are different. When this happens, it is important to relieve the tension between the two by either making shifts in your program or revising the values stated here. This will cause serious reflection, and the cognitive dissonance that ensues may actually be uncomfortable. That is okay. This is what it means to be a reflective practitioner, and it is difficult work.

The Image of the Child in Reggio Emilia

Mara Davoli, the *atelierista* at Pablo Neruda, told me that the *ingresso*, or entryway to the school, makes the first impression on anyone who enters the schools and is very important in communicating with visitors about the work done with children, both how the work is done and why it is done as it is—in short, the school's view of the child and of education. For example, in the *ingresso* at Pablo Neruda one of the walls had a large panel of documentation of student work, while another wall had photos of the teachers and other staff as well as little summaries of projects that were ongoing in each of the three classrooms. A third wall held information about community initiatives. Bookshelves on the fourth wall held books that had comes as gifts from delegations, documentation books from previous years, and more academic books published by Reggio Children. There were places to sit and a few well-maintained plants as well.

When one entered, the *ingresso* immediately demonstrated great care and attention to detail. It also had a comfortable, lived-in feeling, although quite elegant and professional—no primary colored plastic or writing done to mimic children's print. There were no children's handprints or class sets of artwork displayed. There were panels of documentation, using the children's words and work as organized by the teachers and *atelierista* to share the questions explored through their work. The process of inquiry may not have arrived at a concrete answer and may have even raised more questions; however, it was the process that was displayed. Through these documentation boards, the *ingresso* communicated immediately that children were respected and taken seriously here.

Before you read further, take a minute or two to think about the Pablo Neruda *ingresso* as described above. What view of the child is expressed by such a space? In your journal, make a list of words describing the image of the child that might be expressed by an entryway like this one.

In Reggio the child is viewed as strong, powerful, rich in potential, driven by the power of wanting to grow, and nurtured by adults who take this drive towards growth seriously. The curiosity of children makes them question and research the reasons for all that surrounds them. This is childhood, for the schools of Reggio. This image of the child is drawn from educational, psychological, and sociological sources, as well as the everyday experience of children at the Reggio schools. In addition, the image of the child is drawn from the relationships among children and their parents, friends, and extended family that are observed daily. This understanding of children, education, and childhood influences everything that happens in the Reggio schools.

For instance, in Reggio, "wait time," or giving children time to come to their own understandings, is seen as critical to the process of education. Teachers may leave what seems to Americans like a huge amount of time between conversations on a given subject. The students are given the time to make connections to their own world, in their own time, as competent individuals. This is very much in keeping with the Reggio schools' stated view of the child as competent: if we see children as competent to construct their own knowledge, then the children must be given time to do this.

In another example, children in Reggio have access to the bathrooms without adult supervision. If they need to use the bathroom, they do. They may do so with their friends or classmates, but they are not required to go in pairs or as a whole class. If the children need help, they ask for it. They are permitted to decide on their own whether or not they need help. In addition, the environment is geared to the children in the bathrooms as well as in the rest of the school. The sink is at the children's level so they are able to turn on the water and wash their hands without assistance. The tops of the mirrors in the bathrooms at Neruda are hung by small chains—the bottom of the mirror is flush against the wall while the top hangs a few inches out, so that the whole mirror is angled slightly down towards the floor. The mirrors reflect the images of the children while the adults can only see their legs! This is a clear statement about who the bathrooms are for and about children's worth.

These three features of the Reggio programs are just some examples of the way this image of the child is manifested in the practice of the teachers in Reggio. There will be more examples in the chapters to come.

Values in American Schools

While traveling around the United States to share my experiences, I had the opportunity to visit many schools that were well-known and taken quite seriously as places of learning for young children. Many of them had lovely spaces and thoughtful, reflective practitioners who worked with children in engaging ways. And yet there were often significant gaps between the professed view of the child and the actual practice in these schools. I often had the sense that schools had tried to adopt the Reggio view of the child without deeply examining their own values, their cultural context, their setting, and the community of staff, children, and families.

For example, I once received an e-mail from a school I had visited asking me to share "the objective and materials" for a Reggio project I had spoken about (*colore tra le mani*, discussed in chapter 4, page 76). While I appreciated the interest, it is not possible to approach the project this way. The curriculum in Reggio grows from the teachers, children, and families in those schools and from their cultural context. There are not objectives from the outset of a project in Reggio. Teachers are not forced to align their work with standards or readiness guidelines. This is a different way of conceptualizing one's work from the way we think about teaching and young children in the United States. In some ways we must abandon what we think we know about educating young children to permit ourselves and the children the freedom to explore.

Similarly, American teachers often say they see children as competent while creating environments that limit their movement or initiating projects that are driven by what teachers think children should learn. What adults think children should learn usually has no correlation to what children want to learn.

Loris Malaguzzi said that a teacher's goal is not so much to "facilitate" learning in the sense of "making it smooth or easy" but rather to "stimulate" it by making problems more complex, engaging, and difficult. That is something to consider carefully. The work with children in Reggio Emilia is the work of teacher-researchers who are always thinking both about the children and about their own practice and how it reflects their values about children and education.

To do this work, teachers and schools must first examine their views of children and education before proceeding with Reggio-inspired practices. To see the work and try it without first examining your views and establishing a vision is putting the cart before the horse. After establishing a vision, the next step is to look at what already exists at your school and begin asking yourself questions, taking notes, while beginning to move all elements of your school and work with children towards your stated vision. This is easy for me to summarize in two sentences, but the *reggiani* have been working on it since the end of World War II. After more than fifty years, this process is refined, and the alignment between values and manifestation is much greater than in places where this reflective practice is just beginning. Remember that it takes time to achieve that alignment.

I once heard a story told by the director of a child care center in the United States. Amelia Gambetti, who works for Reggio Children and does a great deal of work with American schools, went to this director's school and remained in the lobby for the first thirty minutes. She asked the staff questions like, "What does this communicate about your view of the child?" as she pointed to different elements of the entryway in the school. The director became alarmed, thinking to herself, "What will happen when she sees the remainder of the school?" This story makes me smile because only that straightforward questioning will push your practice forward. Simple questions about how our values and our practice are not yet aligned are often difficult to answer. Many times they involve details of our programs that we have not yet noticed. It is a challenge to recognize that by not taking the time to make choices regarding these details, we in fact have passively made choices that do not reflect our values.

Take a Look at Your Practice

With this in mind, and taking along your responses to the first set of questions on page 14, walk around your classroom and school, making notes to yourself about what you see. Really look at what is there. This is one of the first steps American educators can take towards working in

Reggio ways. Sometimes it is too difficult to really see what surrounds us daily. If so, ask a colleague or friend to come to your school and make notes. They do not have to be early childhood educators to make observations on what they see. Fresh eyes are useful.

As you walk around, take notes for yourself, but try to avoid making judgments. Ask yourself questions about the environment, the routines, the curriculum planning: Why are the plant leaves dusty or limp from lack of watering? Why are there fake plants instead of real ones? Why are many of the toys stored out of reach of children? Could the storage areas be covered to create a more pleasing aesthetic sense? Are there boxes of old materials stored on top of cabinets? Why do the children eat on paper plates? Why is the food made the previous day and reheated?

These sample questions come straight out of notes from centers I have visited in the United States. They certainly do not apply to all centers, but some questions of this type will apply to your center. Here are some others: How are materials presented? Is the restroom accessible to children at all times? Is the documentation at an adult's eye level or a child's? Where do the children eat? Where do they rest? What do they rest on? Is the outdoor space cement with a play structure? Is there adequate natural light? Does the air move freely throughout your school? Are there mirrors for children to see themselves?

Whatever their answers to the more complex questions you discussed in your journals, any early childhood educator in the United States would likely say they see children as having value. If we say we view children as having value, we have to ask ourselves what the value we place on children looks like on a day-to-day basis. Try to see your space from the viewpoint of a child. Get on your knees and walk around. Look up: What do you see? Look at the walls. Are they stimulating? Are they orderly? Clean? What are the clothes like in the dress-up area— adult hand-me-downs or child-sized fantasy clothes? In the house-play area, are the kitchen implements real or from a kitchen kit for children? Does the environment hold your attention? Do you want to stare at the light sparkles made from a hanging prism? Are musical instruments available? Are there places for the children to interact with one another both inside and outside? Are there safe "nooks" for two or three children to go to on their own? How are the blocks in the construction area stored? Is there a construction area? House-play? Dress-up?

These are sample questions; you will be able to think of many others that are relevant to your setting and program. Make careful notes to yourself, knowing that you will revisit them throughout the book. This is not the time to begin with criticism but instead to begin opening up possibilities.

Real-Life Examples

In working with teachers from a number of different parts of the United States, I have seen many programs begin working through questions like those asked above. Here are a couple of examples of programs' discussions and the compromises they reached to begin aligning their values with their practice.

In one school the director and owner both made strong cases for their view of the child as competent and valuable. Many things about their program reflected this value, but mealtimes and rest time seemed problematic. The children ate off paper plates in shifts, in groups of fifteen at a time. Once they were finished, they moved to the rest area to rest while other children took their turn to eat lunch.

These practices raised many questions as we observed, but the most obvious was about the plates. Why did the children eat on paper plates? Was it possible to use plastic or ceramic plates that could be washed? What did paper plates communicate to children about their value?

There is a notable difference in a meal served on a paper plate versus something more substantial. It is like being on a perpetual picnic. It directly affects the ways students behave, the amount of food eaten, and the treatment of the eating area. Overall, it changes the nature of mealtime to something hurried and unimportant.

In discussion, we discovered that the teachers thought using ceramic plates would create too much clean-up work and were worried about children dropping plates and breaking them. Nonetheless, they clearly saw the importance of changing the most basic elements of the lunch routine to create something more significant, in keeping with their declared view of children. When I left, they were working on ways to put into practice their view of children as valuable and competent.

In this same school we discussed the way the children rotated to the rest area while some children still ate. Was it possible for all of the children to get a real rest with so much activity going on while they were trying to settle down? The conversation that ensued brought up issues of management and convenience for the teachers. At the same time, the discussion kept returning to what they had stated as their view of the child and their vision of a school for young children. Teachers recognized that if the management of the children was going to take precedence over the development of the children, then the vision would need to be revisited. The staff recognized that these are not small changes to make, but they were receptive and eager to begin because they saw that the benefits to the children would be enormous.

Beginning the Change Process

As these examples show, in order to work with authenticity, it is not enough to define your view of the child—you must also work to put this vision into practice. This is no small task, but once it takes root, the program will be a powerful manifestation of well thought-out values. Take some time to look at the answers to those first questions about your view of children and education, and compare them to your observations of your own school.

Go back to your notebook and read over your observations. Then look over the answers you provided to the questions articulated by Carlina Rinaldi. What do you see? First, look at the places where your view of the child is reflected in your program. Make sure you take note of the things you are already doing that are in alignment with your vision. I am sure there are many.

Now make a list of five aspects of your program that do not reflect your values about children. Five is enough to start with. Have you said you see children as independent, but the children do not have independent access to the restrooms? Perhaps there is a way to hang mirrors so you could see the children in the bathroom and then leave it open for their access and exploration. Do you believe children construct their own knowledge, yet the school is not print-rich with books and magazines at a level accessible to children? Perhaps you could begin to place baskets of reading materials in a variety of places around the school—in the entryway, bathrooms, common area, and so forth—so children can get to them as desired. Did you say childhood is about exploration and discovery, but the materials are put away at the end of each day? The children may need several days to complete a painting or construction project. Perhaps you can find a way to leave their work on the easel or in the block area for days in order for them to revisit it. Or if this is not possible, perhaps you can photograph or draw their work from one day so they can use it as a departure point the next time they come to school.

This list-making will take some thought and time. Give yourself the time to do so. Share your lists with a colleague, and ask her opinion on what parts of your program do not reflect your values. Sit with it for a while. This part of your exploration will probably take weeks or even months, and the examination of your program in light of your values will continue as long as you work with children. That is not to say you cannot continue to read and reflect, but spend the time necessary to lay the proper foundation upon which you will work. The questions posed by Carlina Rinaldi will not be answered in one sitting or even several. You may answer the first one or two and think about others. Then you will tour your school and take notes on one day and then another, perhaps with colleagues on different occasions. The idea here is to gather information to inform your views and practice. Take the time necessary to do so.

Once you have written your list of five, rank them in order of importance. We will continue to return to this list throughout the book as a vehicle for your professional development. Over time, as you become more comfortable with the process of questioning yourself and looking at your program, you will revise this list, subtracting items as you take care of them and adding others. Soon, the process of questioning, reflecting, and resolving the conflicts between your values and your practice will become second nature to you.

It has been said that the environment should act as a kind of aquarium which reflects the ideas, ethics, attitudes and cultures of the people who live in it. This is what we are working toward.

—Loris Malaguzzi

Chapter 2

Space and Environment

n talking about the physical space that surrounds children in the schools of Reggio Emilia and Reggio-inspired programs in the United States, it's necessary to distinguish between two facets of the same thing. For clarity I am using the terms *space* and *environment*. *Space* refers to the physical, unchanging features of the place in which one lives and works with children—doors, windows, access to the outdoors, and so on—and the inherent values about children and education these features reveal. I recognize that for many early childhood programs, the space is simply what is available; nonetheless, it is worth looking at with a critical eye. The *environment,* in contrast, is the way this physical space is dressed up, lived in, defined, and redefined over time—the nuances, memories, and suggestions of the spaces we create for children; it is the way the space is used, the lived environment. To understand the difference between these two terms, consider what it might be like to visit two homes with the same floor plan. While the structures (the spaces) are exactly the same, the ways they are lived in (the environments—textures, smells, furnishings, and details) may be completely different. One might be pleasant, and the other less so, depending on the choices of items, artifacts, and comforts that define the personality of the space—or they both might be pleasant and inviting but in completely different ways and to different people. The space itself contributes to the environment, but the environment is much more than the space. Another way to think about this is to conceive of the space as forming the scaffold or framework upon which we create the environment.

Please remember that we are using these categories to look at aspects of an organic process that cannot truly be separated, but we are doing so for clarity and efficiency. In this chapter you will look back at your list of values about children and education, using them to analyze the physical space in your program. You will look at how the Reggio view of the child is reflected in the spaces in the schools in Reggio, and you will make some plans about adapting your spaces to reflect your values. Once you have considered the space in your program, you will move on to think about the environment in Reggio and in your program.

Space

The space is made up of windows, doors, hallways, and especially common spaces, such as the outdoor play spaces, the entryway to the school, the bathrooms, the kitchen, and the eating area for the children. The thoughts put into creating this space are important and deserve examining. Is the school constructed with attention to the height of the windows so the children can stand and look outside? Is there ample light and fresh air? Is it a building with rooms connected to hallways or rooms connected to each other, which creates a larger sense of community? Is there a space for the children to gather together? What has been created as a place for children to eat? What is the kitchen like?

Reflecting on Your View of the Child

What are you unconsciously communicating about your values of the child based on the spaces you create? The space is the first step in embodying the vision you clarified in the exercises in chapter 1. The physical features of a space for children immediately communicate a view of the child and the value placed on children and their education by the people who created the space. For instance, at Nido Bellelli, the classrooms had sliding doors that were easy for children to open, while the adult rooms (lounge, lunchroom) had doors that swung open and closed, easier for adults to open than for children.

Take a moment to make a few notes in your notebook about the physical space for children that might embody the values about children and education you discussed in the first chapter. Ask yourself questions like these:

- What type of space is ideal to facilitate the exploration and learning of small children? Please describe it physically in detail.
- Now take that question even further. If you had unlimited resources, what would this space be like? Would the ceiling roll open to bring the sun indoors? Would there be a room for making and firing ceramic projects? A shallow pool outdoors for water play? Would it have a kitchen built at child level for children to cook?
- Be sure to consider all the details of this space. Would it have hallways? Sliding or swinging doors? What would the doors be made of? Don't forget to include the bathrooms, meeting spaces, and outdoors.
- Think again about the view of the child you expressed in chapter 1. How is this view of the child represented in the space you have described? Are there any parts of your values about children that are not yet expressed in the space? Ask yourself specifically how the space can support the

qualities you described, and develop your description until you are sure that all aspects of your values are represented in the space.

As you are writing, notice where you become uncomfortable or what kinds of barriers you automatically create. What are your own limits—for example, in terms of safety, control, organization—in creating a space of this nature? Would doors without latches be too free? A shallow pool too risky?

Looking at Your Space

With these ideas in mind, draw a map of the space in which you currently work. This will be the point of departure from which you will examine your own space and environment in the following pages. Be sure to include all the details.

- Doors
- Windows
- Bulletin boards
- Electric outlets
- Water sources
- Documentation panels
- Classroom areas (house-play, music, library, blocks, and so on)
- Bathrooms
- Entryway
- Outdoor spaces

You will make this basic floor plan more detailed later.

As you work on your floor plan, consider questions like these, and jot down a few notes about them in your journal:

- What spaces make up your classroom?
- Are you satisfied with what is offered? Why or why not?
- What options are presented to children in each part of the space?
- Please list a few possibilities for engaging children in each space. These may be based on how you see children using the space, or other possibilities you can imagine.
- How does the space reflect the values you have stated for your school? Which experiences do you believe children have a right to explore?

- How might it be possible to rotate particular spaces into existence and then out during the school year? Among the many possibilities are music, construction, dramatic-play, house-play, reading, writing, game tables, and group meeting space. Must you have all of these all of the time? Remember that the decision as to what children have a right to explore should drive the organization of the space, which will then be followed by the dressing of the environment.

Space in Reggio

After having worked in Reggio for a number of months, I took a period away from my school, Pablo Neruda, and went to a *nido*. The *nidi* represent the zero to three component of the educational project. Nido Bellelli, where I was placed, is one of four schools that follow the same floor plan. These schools were designed collaboratively by teachers and architects to support the educational vision of the Reggio schools. The building was planned to facilitate communication and to create a space that could be lived in and changed. Teachers had articulated a number of things about the space: no hallways, lots of windows, natural light, the ability to feel the outdoors while inside. The teachers and architects paid special attention to having rooms connect to one another, instead of hallways, to keep the feeling of openness throughout the school. The rooms all open off the *piazza,* or square, which is used as the common meeting space and is the heart of the school. Also, the windows are large and are installed at the appropriate height for small children; they slide open horizontally to literally bring the outdoors inside. The school is so well organized that its educational project is tailored perfectly to the space. The educational project drove the original definition of the space, and the project and the environment keep each other in check over time.

All four schools built to this plan have their own personality and feel, but they all are within the same educational project and spring from the same vision. For example, the bathrooms were built with the same child-sized toilets, but at Nido Bellelli there is a mirror hung from the ceiling above the changing table so the children could watch and engage themselves while having their diapers changed. At Arcobaleno, one of four *nidi* similar to Bellelli, the teachers did not hang mirrors in this way. The space at Arcobaleno is lived differently.

Once while taking a delegation on a tour of Nido Arcobaleno, we stopped in the *lattanti* sleeping room. In the place of cribs, there were *cestini*—woven baskets lined with padding and covered with fabric for the children's comfort. On one side of the *cestini* there was a gap that was about 8 inches in diameter and created a sort of doorway into the basket. While looking in this room, one of the visitors remarked that the children could get out of the *cestini* with the doorway on the side. My Italian colleague smiled and responded that that was the point! If the children awoke they could move about, socializing with one another, or they could seek out the adults instead of being confined to their cribs and crying when ready to get up, which would wake the other children. The *cestini* are used at more than one *nido,* but on that tour they provided a striking contrast to the environment at Nido Bellelli. In looking at this room and touring the remainder of the school it was difficult to recognize that the underlying floor plan was identical to that at Nido Bellelli. The lived environment was so different that it seemed as if one were in an entirely different building altogether.

In Reggio all the schools are different. Some are in old houses, others in more recent constructions. However, each school has these elements:

- Atelier
- Kitchen
- Group meeting space that might double as the lunchroom and rest area
- An entryway, however small

Each classroom has these elements:

- A construction area
- An art area, be it a mini-atelier or tables that double as something else
- House play/dress up
- Reading/library area
- Tables for games
- Bulletin boards

At many schools each classroom also has computers.

In Reggio, the space is made to respond to each group of children and teachers. Paola, one of my mentoring teachers, once told me that a perfect space would be totally redefinable and not limited by the space or furniture. It could be redone at any time to include elements like music, art, or physical play, depending on the needs and desires of the children and teachers. Her class might use one room for construction, while the next group to live in the space would find the area served better for house play or theater. For this reason, the considerations that went into the actual construction of the space were critical. In her classroom, if there were no furniture, one would see endless possibilities. As with most other classrooms, there are hardwood floors, many windows, and simple, clean, white walls. The rooms initially struck me as stark in some ways. But over time I grew to appreciate the clean lines and understated calm of the rooms. The school itself did not jump out at the children but instead offered a place for the students to hang their experience. The classroom served as a canvas upon which the students and teachers could create their own body of work.

The teachers and *pedagogisti* of Reggio Emilia have contributed a great deal of thought on educational spaces, which is worth investigating for further direction. The work of Vea Vecchi, the *atelierista* for many years at Diana, is particularly interesting. Signora Vecchi has been fundamental in the development of the Reggio Approach, having served as the first *atelierista*. She worked directly with Loris Malaguzzi and was the *atelierista* at the Diana preschool for over twenty-five years. She has literally defined and redefined many elements of the approach through her practice at the Diana school. Signora Vecchi has gone on to work with the development of environments and spaces within which the learning of young children occurs, using her experience at the preschools to further the discussion on the possibilities for these environments. For examples of Signora Vecchi's work, see *Children, Art, Artists* (Reggio Emilia, Italy: Reggio Children, 2004) or *Theater Curtain: The Ring of Transformations* (Reggio Emilia, Italy: Reggio Children, 2002), which discusses a project for which Signora Vecchi was the *atelierista*.

Let's look at one component of the Reggio space and try to understand how the space expresses the underlying view of the child that drives the program. In the United States, bathrooms for young children are probably the least-thought-out, most-neglected spaces in the schools I have visited. When we ignore the bathrooms, what does this communicate about the way we view children, especially to the children? In Reggio Emilia, on the contrary, the bathrooms are well-manicured spaces that facilitate connections and relationship building among children. Paola told me that bathrooms are meeting places for children to cultivate relationships and explore in a small comfortable surrounding. The bathroom at her school is completely child-friendly, with the things children use made for their size: for example, sinks lowered to be within their reach, mirrors tilted so children could view themselves from their height. The bathroom is another place to be, another part of the classroom. Similarly, in the four-year-old classroom, the bathroom has documentation on the walls, at child height; a shell collection for little hands; and a big overstuffed chair to sit in with friends and read. There are plants and mirrors and a sink the children can reach without the help of an adult or a stool. Some students go into the stalls in pairs.

Bathrooms are where we spend a great deal of time, and their organization communicates a great deal to children about the business that takes place there. We often wonder why children go to the bathroom to misbehave. Could it be because we have communicated to them that these are neglected, hidden spaces?

Creating Change in Reggio

Nido Bellelli is an educational space created by teachers for teachers and children—still, the building is over twenty-five years old. As a result of the passage of time, the needs of the families and teachers have changed. While I was there, the teachers were working on a project to examine the bathrooms. I asked Lucia why this was being done, thinking in my American way, "Will they renovate?" "Are new toilets coming?" "Have the laws changed?"

Instead, Lucia told me that this project was to redefine the space. It was an opportunity for the teachers to work on a project together as professionals. They were asking themselves to work in the same ways they asked of the children. There was no ending point or particularly tangible goal aside from the process itself.

To begin with, the teachers at Nido Bellelli asked themselves, "What is our bathroom now?" How is it used?" "In what ways does it work, and how does it not work so well?" Lucia and her colleagues sought as a group to define how the bathroom was functioning at that time before they began to think about how it might be changed. Despite the friendly, child-centered nature of the bathroom at Nido Bellelli to the American eye, in some ways the bathroom was not working well for the community of children, families, and teachers at the school at that time.

Once the teachers had defined the bathroom currently in terms of the colors, storage, spaces, and fresh air, among other factors, they moved to the next questions that gave shape to the project: "What do we want it to be?" and "What are the possibilities for a bathroom for young children?" For this component, they again asked themselves, as well as parents at drop off or dismissal rather casually, what they thought of the bathrooms. They consulted architects and books to help understand and explore the possibilities. It was the first place parents arrived when dropping off their children in the morning, and it needed to be functional and welcoming. They explored many possibilities. Would the bathroom become a water park? How could they support the water play while still having a functional space for teachers and parents to use? What was important for the functionality of the bathroom while still making it enticing for a young child? No final decision had been made when I left Reggio. When I asked about the outcome, Lucia laughed and told me that nothing may ever happen but they were using inquiry to push themselves as professionals. The bathroom had simply been the vehicle. You can use the same thoughtful process of inquiry to create change in your spaces to make them better reflect your view of children and education.

Examining Your Space

Take out the floor plan of your classroom or school that you created earlier, and look at what is offered at your school. Ask yourself questions like these:

- What options are presented to children through the organization of the space? Are there enough choices? Are there too many?
- Can the children move easily through the school?
- How are children using the room as it exists? How does the structure aid their exploration? How does it get in their way?
- How might the space itself open possibilities to the children?
- Can the children project their ideas into the rooms, or are they preorchestrated, leaving little room for reinterpretation?

Sometimes less really is more, especially at the beginning. You can always add to your space. At this point you want to make sure it is clean and uncluttered enough to begin developing the environment that will inhabit it.

Changing Your Space

Having reflected on both what exists in your space and what it offers, choose one thing to change. This may be something as simple as repainting to a more neutral tone or moving a classroom area from one place to another to support the way you notice children using the room. At this point you may want to make a list of several changes that might take place, but choose one to begin working on. Changing your space is an evolving process, and one change may lead to others that cannot be anticipated currently or may resolve other needs on the list. The first things you think of may be too large to change immediately (for example, the placement of doors and windows) or might need to be thought through over time (for example, a change that will affect not only your space but others around it, or that will have more than one effect on your space). Be satisfied with making a short list, and then turn your attention to what is in the space, which constitutes the environment.

Be sure to keep in mind that changing the way you think about your space is a process. Making this list is only the beginning. Once you begin asking questions, it will be difficult to limit the possibilities. Allow yourself to make change over time, not all at once. Try one thing, observe how it affects the flow of the day, and go from there.

Approaching the organization of space in this manner creates a living, breathing space that offers endless possibilities for children and adults alike. The key is to make small changes, reflect on them, and perhaps make others. Like little turtles we will progress towards our goals slowly but surely, with small consistent steps over time.

Ambiente or Environment

Now that you have considered the physical space of your program, it is time to look at the second factor, the lived environment. The word *environment* translated directly from English to Italian becomes *ambiente*. In English, a closer word would be *ambience*, which means something somewhat different from environment. However, these are closer in meaning in Italian. Although we talk about the environment in terms of the materials, equipment, and enhancements that create it, what we are trying to create is less tangible than the pieces we use to create it. It is the way a room feels in its entirety, the way it looks but also the way it smells and sounds, the way the air moves through it, whether it is warm or cold, whether it invites us to linger or encourages us to pass quickly through. When you think of the term *environment*, as it will be used in this text, you may want to keep the word *ambience* in your mind. In this book I talk about environment or the *ambiente* as the setting in which children create their worlds and stories. Creating an environment involves the scents, the movement of air and light, and the arrangement of furniture. I will use the words *ambiente* and *environment* interchangeably in this section to try to convey all of these associations.

The environment sets the stage for children's living at school, as the primary aesthetic experience. When you enter it, a school in Reggio Emilia communicates an essence of vitality. It is open, airy, and clean. When I toured the schools, materials were at child level and were enticing—colorful, orderly, and accessible. This communicated immediately the implicit value of children and embodied the image of the child and the stated vision of the Reggio schools. All environments communicate views about children and education that may or may not be explicitly stated. The environment makes your true values explicit.

Take a moment to reflect on your *ambiente* and the way it is arranged. Are you trying to protect the children from putting things in their mouths by having only large objects available to the smallest children? Are the doors closed when the children are in the room to prevent them from roaming off? These are valid concerns, but not ones that should shape an educational project. I came away from my experience in Reggio Emilia understanding that it was possible to help the children discover and respect the dangers inherent in all environments and to stay aware of these for their own protection. In Reggio this happened without a lot of "No! No! No!"

Here is a story to illustrate this from my time at Nido Bellelli with the *lattanti*. It was Jiacomo's first birthday, and his mother had brought cupcakes to school to celebrate the occasion with his classmates. We arranged the children in chairs around the kidney table where they usually ate. Jiacomo was given a cake with one candle in the middle, and it was lit as we began to sing *Tanti auguri a te* ("Happy birthday to you"). As we sang and watched, Jiacomo reached out to touch the flame of the candle. Barbara, one of the teachers told him no, once. He continued to reach for the flame, and his mother told us to let him touch it—he would need to do so only one time to learn that it would burn. So with his forefinger and thumb he pinched the flame and immediately pulled away and began to cry. His mother attended to him and kissed his fingers as we finished singing and served cake to all of the children.

Jiacomo had not suffered any permanent damage and under the watchful eye of adults had been permitted to experiment and learn.

My own boundaries regarding control and freedom were stretched from my first day at Pablo Neruda. American teachers who want to work with children in the Reggio way have to be prepared for this level of discomfort. I asked Paola and Patty how they remained so calm. Paola explained that, from her experience, the children were smart and safe. The only time a child had been hurt in her class, she had been standing nearby. Her point was that there was no way to completely prevent accidents. Instead of limiting the possibilities in terms of materials, languages, and experiences, they sought to make the children aware of their own wellbeing and help them take responsibility for it. Think how different this is from our American attitude that all accidents involving children must be prevented! How does this value about children and education shape the *ambiente* in our schools? How does it control what we allow children to have access to?

There is no shortcut to creating an enticing environment. It is like your home, a place where you spend a great deal of time. Just as at home you choose furniture and decorations with attention to more than durability and the ease of cleanup, other considerations must guide the creation of an environment that welcomes and stimulates children. As with the space discussed previously, your vision and view of the child are reflected in the environment. In the second half of this chapter you will begin to move towards congruence between your values about children and the *ambiente* you create for them. You will examine components of the Reggio classrooms I worked in. Then you will revisit your values about children, and I will ask you to examine the environment in which you currently work to think about how it reflects or does not reflect those values.

Reflecting on Your View of the Child

Think about what you remember of your experiences in school. Think of your favorite teacher or your favorite class from elementary school—what was it like? Can you remember the smells and the feel of the classroom? I think of Mrs. Souza in fourth grade. Her classroom seemed to be an extension of her. It was warm and smelled inviting. We had traditional desks, but we could also sit on big pillows and bean bags in a corner, which created privacy for reading or secret conversations. We had the freedom to make instant soup at snack time. The taste of powdered chicken noodle soup still takes me back to fourth grade.

In your notebook, write a few sentences about that favorite teacher and classroom. Using this as your starting point and looking at what you wrote in chapter 1, answer some of the following questions:

- What kind of feeling do you want to give your students?
- What do you think they need and deserve?
- How should your students feel when they arrive at school?
- How would you like them to live their days: moving about freely, comfortable and independent? Having access to things that interest them? Can they go to the bathroom if they need to?
- How is the school different on a sunny day or a stormy day? Do your students feel safe inside and outside?

Looking at Your *Ambiente*

With your answers fresh in your mind, look around your school again. What do you see when looking carefully at the details? Is it an environment for both children and adults? Do both children and adults live well there? Is it engaging? Using your map, make notes to yourself about what is in each of the areas of your classroom. What kinds of toys, games, and books are there? Are the elements of the classroom cared for and lovingly used? Regularly cleaned and organized?

Take some time to flesh out your map with details: How is the house-play area created? Are there game tables? Is there a substantial construction area, a reading area, a place for group time and places for individual time, an atelier or mini-atelier, outdoor space, a place for music, documentation panels, a class identity card, bulletin boards for parents? I know that thinking about creating all of these features can raise economic issues; however, in Reggio there were many things donated by families or recycled and used in the school. The materials were simple but real.

Ambiente in Reggio

In Reggio Emilia the needs of the children are foremost in the discussion. Here is a story from the time when I was working as an interpreter for an American delegation at the Nido Bellelli. We arrived at the section of the *lattanti* and *piccoli,* the youngest children at the school. Each group of children had its own classroom, and there was a shared *piazza,* where the children met and played together. Next to this, a small garden with a wall of glass permitted light to flood the common play area and created a warm and luminous space in the mornings. A mobile was hung near the glass wall quite high in the air, above the reach of the children, near the eye level of the adults. A member of the delegation asked, "Why is that hung so high if the children here are the youngest and cannot see it or appreciate it?" Lucia, a thoughtful and gentle educator, responded with a smile, "When the sun comes through the windows in the morning, the crystals in the mobile create a light show on the floor for the children." Lucia then reached up and gave the mobile a flick, indicating with a nod the space on the floor splayed with light. This has remained in my mind as a good example of the thought and attention given to what is placed in the environment to enhance it for the children. This mobile was thoughtfully added to the classroom as a subtle *provocazione* of the children. It invited wonder, curiosity, and investigation.

Four ways of thinking about the environment affect all the schools in Reggio and are helpful for American teachers to consider. (Please remember that these categories emerged from my observations and notes, and are not necessarily seen as foci by the adults in Reggio schools.)

- Environment as the third teacher
- Continuity and change
- Public versus private space
- Care and cleaning

ENVIRONMENT AS THE THIRD TEACHER

"The environment as the third teacher" is used almost as a catch phrase by teachers talking about the Reggio schools, but it is not as often examined to see what it really means, both in Reggio and in the United States. Take a moment to write your thoughts in your notebook about this statement. What could the idea of the environment as the third teacher mean?

I did not fully understand what this phrase meant until well into my experience as an intern. Of course, the first and most obvious meaning is the way the students are supported by the environment so that they can pursue their interests and explorations without the interaction or direction of a teacher. But it seemed to have more subtle shades of meaning as well.

For example, let's look at how the environment supported the work of Fabio, a new student who came to Pablo Neruda at four years old and joined the class a couple of weeks into the second year. At this point the four-year-olds had been together a year already. After the morning assembly, the students would each begin to work on whatever projects were of interest to them. They had communicated this to the teachers at the end of the assembly as the teachers negotiated numbers of children per project and wrote down who did what. During this time, for his whole first week, Fabio was literally running, running, running from section to section and project to project, seemingly trying to consume all of his choices and his newfound freedom at once.

Fabio came up to me at the end of his first hectic week and asked, "Julie, what am I supposed to do?" I responded, "Well, Fabio, what do you want to do?" He looked at me with wide eyes and said, "I don't know!" When I related this anecdote to Paola, she laughed and said she had seen this before. She told me that having so many choices presented to the student in the environment made things difficult for one who was not accustomed to such freedom, but Fabio would adjust and calm down. Paola pointed out that it was much more difficult for students to manage their own interests when presented with a number of choices than it was for us to manage these things for the children. It is much easier to be told what to do and to have your time scheduled for you than to do it on your own, especially at age four. The environment was set up and organized, however, to make it easier for children to pursue their interests without the need for adults to manage children, the space, or their time.

Just as Paola said, Fabio did come to accept and live in his environment with calm a few weeks later. At first, it was as if he were set loose in a candy store with five minutes to grab whatever he could. But when he realized there was no rush and he could take his time with the options around him, he did. This illustrated to me how far the children in this class had developed in terms of managing their interests and the choices presented to them by the environment, and the ways in which the environment supported that process.

In Reggio it is understood that the environment should support the work and interest of the children without constant adult guidance and intervention. The children work in the spaces, and while the adults are present, the children build their stories there. The environment is set up with enough provocation to fuel the children's worlds and minds.

CONTINUITY AND CHANGE

The concepts of continuity and change are present in the Reggio schools from the classrooms themselves to the documentation panels to the trees and play equipment in the yard. The members of the school community make an effort to leave behind projects done by groups of students or equipment donated by groups of parents. At the same time, attention is given to what needs to be packed up in order to make room for new students to live there. There is always possibility for redefinition and change.

For instance, when Paola and Patty moved upstairs to the five-year-old classroom, there was a little, open room outside the classroom door that had been used for musical instruments by the group of children who had occupied the space the year before. For Paola and Patty this became the area for books and reading. They draped scarves and put out pillows as well as neatly arranged a selection of books to create a warm, inviting space for children to read.

When it comes time for the classes to rotate to their new homes, the notion of creating *tracce,* or tracks, for the students to begin inhabiting their new space is introduced. There are noticeable tracks of previous students all over the school in the form of projects and their products, which still inhabit the school. For example, at Neruda, a six-foot-long airplane made by children some six or seven years earlier still hung in the four-year-old classroom as well as panels of documentation that could be dated back a number of years. There were representations of many children who currently lived in the spaces and who had passed through the spaces in times gone by.

While visiting with Giovanni, the *atelierista* at La Villetta, I inquired about a project with numbers that had been completed years earlier. In this project, footprints and sequential numbers had been placed on each stair, under a sort of tape or laminate that permitted years of walking on and cleaning them. The numbers began on the first floor and increased as they went upstairs. Giovanni indicated that the footprints and numbers would stay as long as they liked it, as long as it fit with the children and environment of the school. There might come a group of children who wanted to extend or re-explore some element of the project. In that case it might be revisited. Otherwise, it could remain until it no longer worked in the space, and this would be determined by some conversation in the future. This seemed to me to be a perfect example of the tracks children leave within a school.

PUBLIC VERSUS PRIVATE SPACE

In Reggio there is also a small, implicit division between public and private space. Children have cubbies that are considered their private space, the place to put toys from home or things to take home. This space is theirs individually, privately. If their things come out of the cubbies, at least in the classrooms where I worked, they come into the public domain and are to be shared. This notion is also common to American preschools. However, since these little children are still learning about public and private, the Reggio schools set up a structure to scaffold the ideas of public and private so that children could begin to recognize that not everything was in their domain. For example, there are of course what I call "cubby bandits," children who raid the cubbies of others. When this happened with the four-year-olds, the situation was brought out in the public forum for discussion by the entire class. The children learn what it means to have their own private space and respect the private space of others through inquiry and discussion. Isn't this what we want to do as schools, to help children experiment with the world, thereby constructing a tool kit of strategies they are able to use later? It makes me think of John Dewey's statement, "Experience is education," a simple but profound concept that is practiced in Reggio Emilia.

CARE AND CLEANING

At the end of my full-time year as an intern, we stayed at the school for a week after the children left. I was unclear as to why until arriving the Monday morning after the children had finished school. We had coffee, and then I was recruited to roll up my sleeves and work with the staff on the end-of-the-year cleaning. We moved every piece of furniture, washed every toy by hand, wiped down every surface—it gave new definition to the term *spring-cleaning!* The furniture was stacked to the side so the floors could be polished over the remainder of the summer.

The way the school is cared for both during the school year and particularly at the end made an impression on me. It is not a matter of just packing things away to be dealt with in August; the school is stripped and cleaned. I might have anticipated something of the sort considering the manner in which the school is maintained during the school year. It is clean, free of dust, cared for. The plant leaves are dusted, surfaces washed, linens done weekly. The school is treated as one would one's home environment. This ties directly into the Reggio view of children and what sort of environment they merit.

Revisiting Your *Ambiente*

In thinking about the environment in which you work, list a few things that are not working well for the children, whether or not they are working well for you. List five adjectives that describe your environment. Then write down five words that describe what you would like it to be. For example, perhaps the chairs are child-sized but uncomfortable, and the children prefer to sit on the floor. Perhaps the children need adult help to access paper, pencils, or other art materials. Perhaps they are not able or not allowed to turn on the sink by themselves.

After thinking about and reflecting on the responses to the questions posed in the previous pages, you can now make changes to the environment in which you work. When making these changes, look carefully at the vision expressed at the beginning and, if necessary, revise and recopy your responses.

As you think about creating the environment within your school space, consider the following:

- Furniture (child-sized, welcoming, cared for)
- Tools (real-life instruments for house play and dress up, wooden and metal pieces for construction)
- Lighting (use of natural light, low lighting, colored light)
- Provocations (see chapter 4; mirror triangle, light table, prisms, toys, animals hanging on elastic directly from the ceiling)

- Mirrors
- Sounds (piano or other musical instrument, music, music makers)
- Window coverings
- Settings for children's work (for example, a wooden foundation to build on so the work has a frame)
- Fabrics, scarves
- Colors

This list is just an introduction to the kinds of considerations you will use to create your lived environment according to your taste and your view of children and education.

Try to answer the following questions as you rethink your space:

- How is your environment serving the children as the third teacher?
- Are children able to engage the environment without an adult intermediary?
- Is it *provocante?*
- Does it stimulate children individually and in groups? How?
- Does the setting support or limit social interaction? How?

Creating Change in Reggio

When I first started in the four-year-old section, Paola and Patty were unhappy with the way the children were using the construction space. They began with a simple question: "How are the children using the space now?" After careful consideration and note-taking for a few days, they answered that mainly boys were using it, individually and in small groups, and that it was trafficked for short periods of time as opposed to longer periods.

Next, they asked themselves how they wanted it to be used. They wanted it to be trafficked by more girls, by larger groups of children, and for longer periods of time. The idea was to optimize the space for the children who lived there currently as opposed to continuing with the space and definition of this space that had worked with other groups of children in the past. This also exemplified the way the teachers work in the ways that they are asking the children to work: asking questions, hypothesizing, testing, and then looking at the results.

Paola and Patty understood that in order to use the construction space differently, they would have to change it. Paola had the idea to project nature scenes on the wall as a backdrop behind the construction. This was their point of departure. After we started projecting the nature scenes, we noticed the children were building differently. They had begun to build vertically—their structures used the scenes as a backdrop, and they tried to fill the height of the space created by the light. From this observation, Paola brought in a slide projector that changed the background more frequently and watched how it affected the children's construction. Paola also pointed out that groups of girls were building together in response to the trees and florals projected on the wall, and that children were occupying the space for longer periods of time.

This process was a powerful example of how one small change influences the work of the students. It also demonstrates the Reggio model of teacher as researcher, using the inquiry method with the children and each other.

Changing Your *Ambiente*

Having already made a list of changes for the space, use your map and, looking carefully at your environment, think about what could be changed to move you further along the path of Reggio-inspired practice.

- Are there things that can be done by moving furniture or by rethinking storage?
- Could you throw away materials that you might use "someday"?
- How are the children living in the classroom?
- Are there sections of the class rarely used?
- Are there areas used by mainly boys or girls?
- Are some areas used mainly by groups of children, and others used mostly by individuals? Which ones? Why do you think that is? Does it change at different times of the day?

Choose an area of the environment, and, using the questions above, spend three or four days watching how your students live in the area. Take copious notes about the time frame, the gender, the specific students who frequent the area. Ask yourself the simple question Paola and Patty asked themselves about their construction area, and do not assume that you already know the answer. Look with new eyes to see what is really happening.

At the same time, think about how the environment can begin to be or further serve as the third teacher for your students. Would it be possible to organize materials so students can interact more independently? Be prepared for your own resistance. Although many American teachers sincerely believe that children should and can function independently, we are often unaware of how many restrictions we place on them. This comes from our culture. Be aware of this tendency as you progress.

Shortly after I returned to the United States, I was asked to visit a school and give feedback on the environment. I was taken on a tour of the classrooms, and we discussed the way things were arranged and hung. When we arrived in the room for toddlers, everything was stored in cabinets high on the walls, with the lower part of the wall bare of any decoration or photos. Perhaps most striking was the bathroom. It had a divided door in which the top of the door swung separately from the bottom. The bathroom itself was rather small and clean with a little window, toilet, and changing table. I noticed that the bottom part of the divided door was held closed with a large strip of duct tape. When I inquired why this was so, one of the teachers explained, "Well, the door slams when the children repeatedly open and close it."

We continued the conversation rather delicately. "Why not tape it open so that it doesn't slam and the children have access to the bathroom, which they seem curious about?" I asked. The resistance in the room was palpable. With the *reggiani* in mind, we talked about whether it would be possible to have the door securely open with a mirror placed strategically to view the bathroom even when teachers were far from the door, so the children could be free to go in and out but kept in view. By asking a few questions of themselves, the teachers began to engage in revising their environment to reflect their stated vision.

Continuing to Think about Your *Ambiente*

Once you have created your list of possible changes, keep it available, but do not try to revolutionize your school overnight. Remember that the schools in Reggio Emilia began after World War II. They have had a great deal of time to get where they are. With this in mind, go slowly and thoughtfully, carefully observing the effects the initial changes create. For example, by moving the construction area, you may find that the way the rest of the environment is lived changes significantly. This could mean that the list of things you want to change in your environment is suddenly obsolete. It is important to stay present in the environment the children inhabit, and to regularly observe and reflect on whether it works towards creating your educational vision. As your vision changes, the environment must change as well. Try to do a monthly check-in by taking the time to step outside daily life and observe how this life is lived in the environment provided; then make one or two small changes. If you continue with this regular reflection, the environment will become refined over time to embody your vision more accurately.

Creativity seems to emerge from multiple experiences, coupled with a well-supported development of personal resources, including a sense of freedom to venture beyond the known.

—Loris Malaguzzi

Chapter 3

The Organization of Time

Like the organization of space discussed in chapter 2, a program's daily schedule and the view of time held by the people involved in it are part of the skeletal structure upon which a school is organized. The organization of time gives shape to the day, the projects, and the work of both the children and the adults; it includes drop off and pick up, the time the children are together as a group and independent, as well as outside time, lunch, and rest. The structure determines much of how the school experience is lived: the number of transitions, the feel and flow of the day, and the shape of the work the children do. For instance, if a day is planned around concrete blocks of time that include thirty minutes for art, who is to say that a child can comfortably work within that time frame? Their creativity or ability to engage may take much longer.

Patricia Hunter-McGrath, the *atelierista* from Evergreen Community School in Santa Monica, California, once described a project she did with her students involving a large block of clay placed in the common area. The clay was put there for the children to engage and explore, and engage they did. Photos of the way the students met and negotiated this large block of clay over several weeks were part of the documentation of the experience. Some students immediately jumped on the clay the first day, while others waited weeks before approaching. What if the clay had only been available for a day or two? Not all of the students would have had the opportunity to explore this medium, as their pacing would not have been in keeping with that of the adults who were making the decisions.

Reflecting on Your View of the Child

Instead of modeling ourselves after the schools of Reggio, which will never do since we do not live in the culture of Reggio Emilia, Italy, let us instead glean questions from their work that can then lead us to the appropriate responses for our own programs. Look back at the questions you answered in chapter 1. Remind yourself of your own view and vision before proceeding to the more focused questions below.

Consider the following and write down some notes for yourself before examining your use of time:

- How do young children move through their days? Slowly? Quickly? Are they focused or fluttering about from one thing to another?

- How do children respond to unexpected transitions? How do young children respond to transitions in general?
- If you were to define your ideal day with your students, what would you do? What would it include?

We will refer to these questions as we examine your schedule and use of time. Consider the questions posed in chapter 1, those that give shape to your vision, as the umbrella under which time is placed. As each element of your practice becomes more clearly defined, it must be aligned with your vision. For example, if you believe children can build knowledge, how much time are they permitted to do so? Or realize that if part of your vision states that children are strong and independent, then placing arbitrary time constraints on them that inhibit their strength and independence would be contrary to your understanding of children.

Looking at Time in Your Program

As a point of departure, take a moment and in your notebook write down your school schedule. This can be the schedule you worked with last year or the one you are currently using. Be as clear as possible, and be sure to include the arrival window for children, the point at which the school day begins, how it progresses from there, the transition times and blocks of activity time—everything from the beginning of the day until it is time to go home. If you have more than one schedule, pick the one with which you seem to struggle most for whatever reason—the schedule in which you feel rushed or notice harried or resistant children, the one that stumbles instead of flows. You may already notice ways in which your schedule and the values you wrote down above are not congruent. Be gentle with yourself; don't worry too much about fixing that now. Just observe yourself and make notes.

In looking at your schedule make note of the following:

- How many transitions occur during the day? What are these transitions? Play to lunch? Lunch to rest? Group time to art?
- How long are the arrival and departure windows? Ten minutes? Thirty minutes? An hour?
- List the number of activities that are scheduled from arrival to departure.
- Do the children have any unscheduled time?
- How long are the different components of the day? Write the times per section of the schedule on your schedule.

Time in Reggio Emilia

On my first day at Pablo Neruda, Mara Davoli, the *atelierista*, took me around the school to look at the space and then to introduce me to the class where I would work. As we arrived in the four-year-old classroom, the children were running around and socializing. One of the teachers was speaking to a parent, and the other was engaged with a small group of children in an adjacent room. Mara began, "This is the four-year-old section. The school day begins around nine, but there are no bells, so give or take a few minutes. . . ." I noticed that it was actually a few minutes after nine, and as Mara took me around the classroom, the teachers began to gather up the children—gently, softly—to begin the day.

What are the values imbued in such an approach to time and its management? There was no struggle against the clock or an attempt to fit too many things into a small block of time. It was not a Wall Street office but a school for young children, and that race with the clock was simply not present. The hectic pressure to keep on schedule wasn't there. Things happened in their own time and space without the forced nature a rushed schedule or over-scheduling gives. This held true for discussions, lunch, and rest—it was all flowing and negotiable. Some children ate more slowly, while others needed more rest, and the schedule was elastic enough to accommodate these differences.

First, let's look at a typical day at Pablo Neruda. Then we will break it into components to discuss in more detail.

PABLO NERUDA SCUOLA DELL'INFANZIA TYPICAL DAILY SCHEDULE

7:30–9:00 a.m. Children arrive and play freely.

9:00 a.m. (approximately). Students and teachers gather together for the assembly and to share some fruit. This time together drives the activities of the day. Fresh fruit is distributed, stories read, questions posed, and children allocated into projects for the morning. The assembly can be anywhere from thirty to fifty minutes depending on the day. Again, there is no predefinition.

9:30 to 10:00 a.m. The assembly ends, and students begin to work on projects independently in small groups or with teachers in small groups. On a nice day they may go outside as a class.

11:00 a.m. Students may be working in class or in the yard before lunch. Students are generally self-managed at this point, with teachers engaging small groups or individuals.

11:30 a.m. This is the time to get ready for lunch, with the teachers calling for kids to wash up and meet together to share the morning's activities, as well as set tables and lay out the sleeping mats and blankets.

11:45 a.m. Lunch begins.

12:30 p.m. All students are finished with lunch, although some may finish earlier and be excused to prepare for rest. But by 12:30 all of the kids go to prepare for rest, which means taking off their shoes and washing up again. They jump on the mats near their friends, settling down for rest, which takes ten minutes or so. They often listen to stories on tape as they fall asleep.

3:00–3:15 p.m. By this time the children are awake or are gently roused to join the group for a snack. The children get up, put on their shoes, have a snack, and play freely until their families pick them up.

4:00–4:30 p.m. Pick up begins. Parents drift in and chat with the teachers while the kids play, and the parents get caught up on what happened during the day or visit with other parents. Some children whose parents come closer to 6:00 p.m. participate in an extended day program. At this time they go with a different teacher, and all ages are together for those two hours after the regular school day.

In looking at this schedule, one can see that it is fluid and elastic. The values embedded with relation to time are not simply *reggiani* but Italian. As students move forward in school, however, the schedule becomes more rigorous. Here, with the young children, it is almost as if time is suspended. There are things they do each day and can anticipate, such as assembly, fruit, projects, lunch, rest, snack, and pick up. It all follows in the same predictable order but without fret. The Italians always say, "*domani, domani,*" meaning "tomorrow, tomorrow," essentially communicating it can get done tomorrow, if not today. While that may be lost on some adults, it remains in the preschools of Reggio Emilia. The teachers do not push to finish a project or conversation but plan to finish at an undetermined point in the future. This could be tomorrow or the day after tomorrow or next week. Things are permitted to unfold in their own time. This includes the work done with children as well as the documentation and reflection done by adults. Children are given ample time and space to make connections on their own time.

Now, let's look at each of the components of the Reggio schedule in more detail.

Drop Off

This is a pleasant, informal time of day when students are dropped off at school. Parents often stop to chat with the teachers or play for a while with their children before departing for the day.

Assembly

Assembly is the heart of the educational project in Reggio Emilia. It is in the morning assembly or meeting that the class connects, shares a piece of fruit to begin the day, and discusses all of the things that make up the educational project.

The assembly has a consistent routine, beginning with fruit prepared in the kitchen and distributed by the students while the teachers ask, "Who is missing today?" The students look around and make note of which students are not present. The assembly can then go in almost any direction, from reading a story to playing a guessing game to posing a hypothetical question to the students to asking them about their opinions about a particular topic. The assembly in the three-year-old class may last fifteen minutes with fruit, an inventory of who is missing, and perhaps an examination of paintings done the day before or an exchange of messages the students have created. The assembly becomes increasingly longer as the students age, with the five-year-olds engaging in lively, focused discussions that can last forty-five minutes or more on a variety of topics.

The assembly gives shape to the day. The teachers use this time to plant seeds in the minds of the students and to follow up on discussions that have taken place earlier. The students talk and are listened to, and the teachers take notes on what is said or tape-record the conversation to transcribe later. Universally in the Reggio schools, at the end of the assembly students make choices about which of the offerings for that day they want to participate in. For example, Paola may say, "Who wants to go to construction?" Three or four students are chosen from those who express interest. There may be three or four or five things offered, and the students choose what they want to do.

Project Time

During project time the students go to whatever they chose and begin their "work." The students are free to move about and engage in more than one thing; after assembly, they manage their own interests. As the morning progresses, the teachers may invite students into the atelier to work on something, depending on how many students can be accommodated at once. A student may begin in the construction area and then join friends in the atelier to draw or paint and then move on to play games.

When it is almost time for lunch, the class usually gathers once more to share how they spent the morning and what transpired. This is generally a brief meeting to reconnect before going to lunch.

Lunch

Lunch is a sit-down time with cloth napkins and tablecloths, and the children are served a traditional Italian meal consisting of a first course, usually pasta, rice, or soup, followed by a second course of meat or fish and vegetables. All of the students drink bottled water, and some assist in the set up and cleanup of the lunchroom. The older children serve food to their classmates and bus the tables, while the younger children pick up napkins and take their own plates to the clean-up cart when they have finished eating.

Rest

All students rest after lunch. As the children grow older, some give up their nap, but they still remain in their resting place on mats or small cots to relax after lunch.

Snack/Free Play

Once the students wake up, they gather at tables and have a snack of breadsticks or pretzels and juice while they put on their shoes and finish waking up.

Pick Up

Family members—grandparents and parents—begin arriving around 4:00 p.m. to pick up students. This is a time for students to play freely while teachers and parents visit, discussing individual children or communicating school business. At Neruda parents can consult the daily agenda posted on the bulletin board outside the classroom, which gives a summary of the day's activities, projects, and birthdays. Some days the agenda has digital photos of activities that have taken place.

Four elements of the Reggio approach to time stood out to me and are important for you to think about as you attempt to work with young children in Reggio ways:

- the Italian cultural approach to time
- the use of "wait time" in the Reggio schools
- the need to allow time for children to make their own connections
- the sense of the individual as part of the group

TIME IN ITALY

While living in Italy, I picked up an idiomatic expression, *"domani, domani,"* or "tomorrow, tomorrow." This represents a great deal of what I learned to appreciate about the respect for time in Italy. The Italians are not in a rush to do things. If one encounters a friend out and about, there is always time to get coffee and have a chat. Day planners and PDAs did not rule the days of the people I met. Mealtimes are valued as times to meet, eat, and talk. Lunch is followed by a rest time, during which businesses are closed. Certainly the Italians could maximize their business hours, but that is not the cultural value. The hours spent at leisure and with family and friends are treasured above all else. There is no hourglass sense of time slipping away. What does not get done one day will get done the next. This was a novel and frustrating concept for me initially. Once I learned to let go and work within the more relaxed Italian concept of time, however, my life proved to be less stressful. This approach to time is present to varying degrees throughout Italy. The American concept of time is much different, and it is important to understand and respect our own cultural values around time, but also to be willing to push ourselves a little as we examine the schedules we live in with young children.

WAIT TIME

Before I went to Reggio, my idea of "wait time" was to wait a few seconds beyond my comfort zone before calling on students. In Reggio, however, wait time can be hours or days. Once I asked Paola about a conversation that had occurred during one morning assembly. Paola had asked the children to think about their favorite stories—would these be different if told in the dark or on a stormy day? Would the children enjoy them more or less on a sunny day or whether they were told outdoors? This was part of a project called *Il Segnalibro* (see chapter 5), and Paola was just planting a seed in the minds of the children. I wanted to know if we would be discussing this again the next day. Paola said no, there were other things to do, and it was too soon. She wanted to give the students ample time to consider the question when they read with their families at home and their friends at school.

Another example of "wait time" in Reggio involved the first project I attempted. Paola and Patty and I began a conversation with the children about living in the five-year-old classroom the following year. We talked about creating a space that was welcoming, and we spoke specifically about a large tower with vertical space that was part of the four-year-old classroom. One student, Giorgia, told us we could put something we like up there. We took the students to visit the space as a sort of provocation to get them thinking, and then we moved on to other topics. We left this concept to simmer a few days and then re-broached it. When we brought it up again, the students were ready to discuss, propose, and plan for this space after the extended wait time. These are just two examples of the Reggio way of maximizing wait time to give the students plenty of time to have other conversations about a topic and mull it over on their own.

TIME FOR CHILDREN TO MAKE THEIR OWN CONNECTIONS

The *reggiani* believe children make connections in their own time and each does so individually. With this in mind, refer to the story from Evergreen Community School that begins this chapter. Remember that some children went to the clay immediately, while others waited for weeks before approaching it. The point here is not only that we need to allow children to approach the material in their own time, but also that all the children needed one another as part of the exploration, to construct their own meanings. If the clay had been available only for a day or two, some of the children would have missed the experience, and the thinking of the rest of the children would have been incomplete without the input of those children who were slower to engage. The experience would have been less rich and the learning less deep for all the children. In making meaning, "the reasons, the explanations, the interpretations and meanings of others are indispensable," says Carlina Rinaldi (1994).

I saw this when I worked in the schools of Reggio. When exploring the shape of things with the four-year-olds, which involved looking at symmetry found in nature, flowers and shells and inside of a sliced orange, not all students were ready for the same type of exploration at the same time. Some students engaged in the flower collection, painting, and drawing immediately, while it took others a bit of time and careful observation of the process before they became engaged. As a group they all interacted, however, and their theories and observations about shape affected one another. Learning does not unfold in a linear fashion. All the children have their own meandering paths that collide into one another, pushing each other forward, backward, and sideways. Ultimately they arrive, but each in their own time. In Reggio this is respected and cultivated.

THE INDIVIDUAL AS PART OF THE GROUP

The way time is handled in a program goes beyond the planned schedule. What happens when there are interruptions or challenges to the schedule? How these "interruptions" are handled says a lot about the values of the program and the view of the child that is held there. In particular, unplanned interruptions offer opportunities to scaffold the kind of learning about the individual and the group that we discussed briefly in the last chapter. Here are a couple of examples of how the morning assembly may unfold in Reggio Emilia.

One morning at Pablo Neruda, Davide and Simone were playing in the bathroom sink, filling and emptying containers, making whooshing noises with the water. The boys were very involved, and this was all happening in the time before the day officially began. When it came time for the morning assembly, the boys were invited to join the group. They took a moment or two to finish what they were doing and transition into the classroom.

In my notes that day I wrote, "For me it is difficult to see where to draw the boundaries. . . . Do we make it a water play station and follow their interests or interrupt and ask the children to abandon their play and join the group meeting?" Later in the morning I asked Paola and Patty, the teachers in this classroom, about this issue. Paola told me that water play would certainly be an option for the children, but at the appropriate time. Both teachers said, "We only ask the children to be together for assembly, lunch, and rest, but it is important that they respect that." The children were able to follow their interests, but it was not a free-for-all. There were times and clear indications for group time and individual or free choice time. In many ways this reflects the scaffolding of private and public space we discussed in the last chapter. Group time and individual time exist in part for the purpose of helping children distinguish between the legitimate demands of community and those of the individual.

The same issue arose in the three-year-old classroom while I was there. This time, Luca did not want to participate in the assembly. All of the children were sitting on chairs arranged in a large circle. Simonetta, one of the teachers, put it very simply and effectively: "Luca, that is fine. But if you do not want to join us in the assembly, you may sit on the bench by yourself." (This was a little space just outside the classroom.) Inevitably Luca chose not to leave the group. He was presented with a choice, but an expectation was also established. Because of the manner in which the options were presented, the most desirable choice was clear, and Luca chose to stay with the group. This might not be all that different from how many American schools would handle the same problem. However, what happened next? In assembly that day, there was a discussion on the importance of the assembly and of meeting together to greet one another and plan the day. The teachers stated clearly that this was one of the values that the school held. Luca had challenged the expectation, but through the conversation skills of the teacher, the group came away with a renewed commitment to their morning meeting.

This notion of time is also a question that came up a number of times while I was working as a translator. The teachers in Reggio make it clear that there is a schedule and expectations of the children are established. When I share this anecdote with some of the groups I work with, inevitably the question is asked, "What if a child doesn't want to join the group?" This is looking at it in black-and-white. The children know the expectations and are for the most part respectful of them. In the United States there is often a tacit understanding that tension exists between the individual and the group, and people ask questions about whether what an individual wants is more important than the group. In Reggio it is understood that children also have a sense of being a larger body and participating as its members. The needs of the individual and the needs of the group are not seen as separate, but as interdependent and interactive. As the *reggiani* see it, children need to be part of a group. This need is part of their development and something they want—in fact something we all want as human beings—and so our job as teachers is to help them learn how to get to something they want. Also, the Italians have a wonderful sense of group or community, and this sense is present in the preschools. This part of the culture supports the expectation that children respect and participate in a group context. The children are seen as individuals, but they are also viewed as a body of individuals with a personality all its own. The interconnectedness of the individual to the class, the class to the school, the school to the neighborhood, to the larger community is palpable as part of the culture.

Looking at Your Approach to Time

When we look at our days with young children, we must determine what are the "musts" of our time, because those are the things that will get done. The musts should be a short list compared to the list of possibilities. For example, I know that in working with young children, each day I have a short list of things I must do. The fewer things I have on my schedule, the better. My list of "musts" includes these four things:

- To meet with my children and have some type of group discussion
- To do some project work or individual/group work
- To have something to eat
- To rest

All else, for me, can be considered extra, value added to my day.

With this in mind, and considering the general principles of the Reggio organization of time discussed above, take a moment to think about the things that *must* get done during your school day. There are many things we would like to do, but those fall into a different category. Many service providers are also mandated to include basic activities such as tooth-brushing and snack; those can also be added to one's list of musts but perhaps be folded into the lunch category. Using your journal, make your list of "musts."

There are always other things we would like to do, but those fall in the "should" or "could" category. Make a separate list of these "should" or "could" parts of your schedule in your journal. Then look back at your schedule, asking yourself questions like these:

- What is working about your schedule? What do you like?
- What problems do you see in your current schedule each day?
- How much time do you need on a daily and weekly basis to accomplish your "musts"? (Remember, the "shoulds" and "coulds" are simply value added.)
- Is there anything you want to add?

Here's an exercise to help you think about schedules without having to tackle your own. Playing with someone else's schedule can often give us distance from the circumstances that seem to restrict us to what we've always done and open up new possibilities. Later we will use this information to examine your schedule.

Look at the schedule below. Take a few moments to make notes to yourself on what seems to work and what might not work well. Imagine yourself inside a day that follows this schedule and anticipate moments that would create transitions or might produce confusion or tension. Try to generate at least two or three suggestions for changes to facilitate a more flexible day.

HYPOTHETICAL PRESCHOOL DAILY SCHEDULE

7:00–7:30 a.m. Open center and greet the families by name with a smile.

7:30–8:30 a.m. Breakfast offered to all children; diaper checks.

8:30–9:00 a.m. Morning art for all ages.

9:00–9:20 a.m. Circle time for group 1.

9:30–10:00 a.m. Snack time for all age groups.

10:00–10:30 a.m. Circle time for groups 2 and 3.

10:30–11:00 a.m. Hands-on activities for group 1.

11:00–11:30 a.m. Lunchtime for group 1.

11:30 a.m.–12:00 noon. Lunchtime for group 2.

12:00–12:30 p.m. Lunchtime for group 3.

12:30–2:30 p.m. Naptime for all age groups.

2:30–3:00 p.m. Afternoon snack for all age groups.

3:00–3:30 p.m. Hands-on activities for groups 2 and 3.

3:30–4:00 p.m. Outdoor activities for all ages.

4:00–4:30 p.m. Indoor activities for all ages.

4:30–5:00 p.m. Open-floor activities.

5:00–5:30 p.m. Story tape for all age groups.

5:30–6:00 p.m. Tabletop activities; get ready to go home.

Do you see some places where changes could be made? What are the "musts" in this schedule? What are you considering as you decide what to change? Make some notes about this in your notebook.

As you probably discovered, there are a number of changes that would significantly change the way time is lived at the school. Here are two changes other teachers have suggested:

1. Consolidate groups 1, 2, and 3 into one large group that follows the same schedule. By doing so, the following changes would also be possible:

- A community morning meeting
- A longer period for art
- One lunch period that extends over a longer period of time

2. The schedule could have several larger blocks of time, giving children more freedom of choice and ability to engage the offerings for a period that suits the individual child. For example, the blocks of time might look like this:

8:30–9:30 a.m. Art for all ages.

9:30–10:00 a.m. Snack and morning meeting.

10:00–11:30 a.m. Hands-on activities, outdoor activities, art activities for all ages (a kind of "project time" as in the Reggio schedule).

11:45 a.m.–12:30 p.m. Lunch for all ages.

12:30–2:30 p.m. Rest for all ages.

There are many other possible changes that would provide more flexibility for both the teachers and the students. It is easy to see that a small change, for example, consolidating all age groups, would dramatically change the schedule. With this one change, many teachers are available to support one group of children, opening up possibilities for team teaching. A host of other options are presented to further modify the schedule in keeping with the educational vision of the school as well as the ease of the teachers and students.

Changing Your Schedule

Look back on your school vision from the beginning of this chapter. What have you written that speaks to fluidity and the way the day is lived? Did you include anything about how it feels to be at school? For example, is there an emphasis on a gentle experience for children where the day flows effortlessly and naturally from one part of the schedule to the next? This would be determined in many ways by the schedule, the organization of time. Make a few notes to yourself regarding your ideas and vision of how a school day unfolds.

Keeping in mind the changes you suggested for the hypothetical preschool, look at your own schedule and do the same thing. This requires that you have present in your mind what you already do, what you want, and what will work. Use your vision and your list of "musts," and make a short list of two to three changes that might create larger blocks of time, more fluidity, and fewer transitions. Choose changes that might be implemented easily and immediately. Rank these in order of importance for yourself and your school, and then revise your schedule by integrating one of these changes.

Be careful not to change everything at once, which would create a shock to the system. Instead look at little changes that can be made immediately—"streamlining," so to speak. Each change made will resonate throughout the day, so the key is to make small, incremental changes. The beauty of this is that after reflecting on your values and schedule, you can begin to map out changes that can be implemented over time. This can be the point of departure, and as you live with the changes, they may require you to make new ones in response to changes you observe in your children or families. Each change will create a new reality to examine, and may resolve problems or present new dilemmas. So begin with one change at a time.

As demonstrated through the hypothetical preschool schedule, one change can bring big results. Therefore, it is important to live with each change made for some time before making additional changes. As time passes, continue to observe periods of the day that are tense or difficult for the adults or the children. Notice how much children eat and sleep, in order to inform yourself about the time permitted for these activities. Notice the number and complexity of works created by the children— drawings, paintings, constructions, and so on. Are they rushed? Be sure to make note of these as you continue to fine-tune your schedule and your approach to time, and address them with one small change at a time.

What children learn does not follow as an automatic result from what is taught, rather, it is in large part due to the children's own doing, as a consequence of their activities and our resources.

—LORIS MALAGUZZI

Chapter 4

Progettazione

I n my first weeks at Pablo Neruda, I was looking for projects. I knew a little about the Reggio approach to curriculum through projects but was unsure I would recognize it as it unfolded. I think that my understanding of the Project Approach as it is used in the United States was the first problem—it was too limited and did not encompass all that *progettazione* included. In chapter 2 I discussed examples of teachers asking themselves and each other questions that pushed their work along: Lucia and the bathrooms, Paola and the construction area of her classroom. These projects emerged from a need or a question in their lives as teachers. It is in much the same way that students demonstrate the interest that develops into a project. *Progettazione,* the development of those interests, is the core of the curriculum in Reggio Emilia.

In this chapter I will first ask you to look again at what you believe about children and learning and to examine how your curriculum works right now. You are not yet assessing it, but merely seeing what is there. Then we will learn about *progettazione* in Reggio Emilia and what it encompasses for teachers and students conceptually. I will discuss the *intento progettuale* used in Reggio and follow that by asking you to revise your list of intended projects. Finally, we will examine working in these ways more concretely.

Revisiting Your Values: What Do Children Have a Right to Explore?

When we speak of projects and where they come from we must look at the invisible structure that is in place in the schools of Reggio and is directly related to the *reggiano* view of the child and vision of education.

Reflecting on your view of the child and values surrounding the education of young children, write down in your notebook the things you think young children have a right to explore. This may include books and the structure of books, relationships, communication, identity, the world around them. Please try to keep the ideas large, not themes like the seasons but larger, open topics that can take on multiple levels of meaning and can manifest differently from one child to another or in different groups of children from year to year.

This issue ties directly into the role of school and education in young children's lives. I will repeat a few questions that may help focus your considerations.

- Who is a child?
- What is childhood?
- How do children learn?
- What is the meaning of "to educate"?

These questions will be part of what drives the choices you make in what your students explore. Consider carefully how children learn and what you believe the meaning of *to educate* involves. Depending on your individual answers, ideas for exploration should emerge. I believe children construct knowledge, so I am inclined to choose concepts for exploration that involve the teacher and the student and the world around them. You may be inclined to believe that to educate is to prepare students for what is awaiting them in the future, and this belief would shape the choices you make. The list of what you believe about how children learn and what "educating" means can be extensive. Generate as many ideas as possible now, as you will refine the list later.

Looking at Your Current Curriculum

Here I will ask you to write in as detailed a manner as possible about the curriculum currently in place at your school. What is done with your students? Describe it by going through a day or a week, but record, without judgment, what kind of work is done to engage students. It is important to be clear and comprehensive so that you can see what is working and might be extended for inclusion in your work in Reggio-inspired ways. Be sure to include any annual pieces that may tie to holidays or have particular importance to your school or students. Be sure to answer these questions and any similar ones you can think of:

- How is the curriculum planned?
- Who is involved in the planning?
- Does the curriculum change each year?
- What are your favorite and least favorite parts of it?
- Do you use manuals?
- Is your curriculum tied to state standards?
- Is it considered an academic curriculum?
- Which of the "hundred languages" are most present in the curriculum you currently use? (In speaking of the "hundred languages" I mean any means by which children engage and learn. For example, a few languages

are singing, working with clay, working with wire, dancing, poetry, music, construction, watercolors, papier-mâché.)

- Does it integrate art?
- What topics are addressed?

The answers to these questions will be useful in making choices about the work you will do as this chapter progresses.

Curriculum in Reggio Emilia: *Progettazione*

A great deal has been written about Reggio Emilia and its approach to projects. While I hear frequently that in the Reggio approach teachers let children's ideas blossom, this description is difficult for me to imagine in concrete terms because in my experience the blossoming of ideas takes tending, nurturing, and interaction. Projects are not pulled out of thin air. Much is missing from the general American understanding of the *progettazione* done in Reggio Emilia. It cannot be fully understood with the term *project approach* or with *emergent curriculum*. I will therefore use the Italian term throughout this chapter to emphasize and respect the complexity of the work done in Reggio schools.

Projects are ways of doing work with children that in effect simulate real life. My life is filled with projects—big and small. Your life is similarly filled with projects. These projects may be orchestrating a wedding for 250 people or dinner for a family seven nights a week, but either way they are projects. You and I probably approach our projects differently, but we engage in similar processes along the way. Each requires thought, planning, preparation, and execution, the four pieces of any project in life. This holds true for the work we do with our students. Imagine if we had begun to get the swing of conceptualizing and executing projects when we were just young children? By high school we would have had the follow-through, persistence, and organizational skills that many struggle to develop in adult life. On my first day at Neruda, Mara Davoli paraphrased one of Loris Malaguzzi's sayings: There is no preschool, just as there is no pre-life. Our students are at school and are learning things that will serve them throughout their lives. Malaguzzi likened it to giving children coins that they keep in their pockets to pull out and spend when the opportunity presents itself further down the road. Mara likened them to tools or strategies gained through experience at school that could be called upon later, in different circumstances. Children have stored the experiences to access and use.

In order to start thinking about developing curriculum projects, I will walk you through an overly simplified example for purposes of clarity. Let us say we are dissatisfied with our living room. We must begin with a few simple questions to give shape to the project:

- How is the living room working now?
- What kind of ambience are we trying to create?
- What do we want the living room to be?
- What is it that we specifically do not like? Can that be changed? How?

When we have carefully considered all these questions and talked with each other about it, perhaps the answer seems to be to re-paint the room. Next comes a series of specific questions that deal with the execution:

- Who will do it?
- How much paint will it take?
- What kind of paint should be used?
- When will it be done?
- What materials will be necessary?
- How much will it cost?
- What color would be best?
- Where will we get the paint?
- How much time will it take?
- What kind of preparation will be necessary?

Once we have gathered information and responded to these questions, we will have a better idea as to the parameters of our project. From that point we will break the task down into smaller parts, such as getting the paint, preparing the workspace, and taping off the walls, and in these kinds of small steps complete our project.

This is an example of how as adults we might go about a grown-up project. Work with children in Reggio is very similar, but instead of changing the living room we are perhaps examining what makes planes fly or developing rules a group can live with. The difference is that when we plan to paint a room, we have a concrete idea of the result of the project, where we are going. When working with children, the end result cannot be envisioned at the beginning, because we do not yet have enough information about the children's ideas and we do not yet know which of the hundred languages will be best for exploring them. The thoughtful questioning and reflection upon the children's responses, wait time while ideas emerge, and reflection time among adults are thus even more essential than if we are painting a room.

DEFINING *PROGETTAZIONE*

To understand the concept of *progettazione* according to the *reggiani,* let us see what Carlina Rinaldi (1994) has to say on the subject.

> I would like to explain why we prefer to use the term *proget-tazione* rather than *curriculum* or *curriculum planning*. We have to consider three important points:
>
> 1. Knowledge-building does not proceed in a linear way, determined and deterministic, by progressive and predictable stages, but rather is constructed through contemporaneous advances, standstills, and retrocession.
> 2. The construction of knowledge is a group process. Each individual is nourished by the hypothesis and theories of others, and by conflicts with others and advances by coconstructing pieces of knowledge and the identities of those who are part of the process. This occurs through situations that provide both confirmation and negation of our hypothesis. Conflict and disturbance force us to constantly revise our interpretive models and theories, and this is true for both children and adults.
> 3. Children produce their own theories, important theories from which they take inspiration. Children possess values, meanings, and times—their own times that both have and give sense and orientation to their processes.
>
> As a result, the term *planned curriculum* (along with corresponding *curriculum planning*) reveals itself to be unsuitable for representing the complex and multiple strategies that are necessary for sustaining children's knowledge-gathering processes.

This is why we prefer to embrace the term *progettazione* to define this complex situation, to describe the multiple levels of action which are definite and indefinite at the same time, that which is carried out in the dialogue between adults and children.

In the Reggio schools an invisible structure exists that can be considered the foundation of the project work done between teachers and students. There is not a scripted curriculum or standards that drive the work in the schools of Reggio. Instead a highly evolved, invisible structure is tightly woven to create the educational project that is Reggio. The components of this structure, as I experienced it, are four types of projects that emerge from different elements of the educational project. The first are the foundational projects based on what children have a right to explore. Next are the environmental projects, then daily life projects, and finally self-managed projects. Many of the *progettazione* in Reggio fall into more than one category.

A school and its staff must decide which project frames, umbrellas, or topics (for lack of a better term in English) they will use as their foundation, the projects based on the things they think children have a right to explore. The framework in Reggio Emilia is called *intento progettuale,* or intended projects, a document created at the beginning of the year that discusses ideas and "appointments" teachers may have with children under larger foundational topics such as color or relationships. *Intento progettuale* is the term for the document that contains topics or themes, which the teachers agree are the main concepts all the children will learn about in a given year. These ideas become the springboard from which they will begin the year and follow the children through the entire three-year experience. The document they create at the beginning will be revisited and shared with colleagues at meetings several times throughout the school year. These "intended projects" may be used over and over with new groups of children as they come to school, or modified over time.

Looking at the *intento progettuale* translated in this chapter, you will see that some of its hypotheses and questions fall outside of the projects that form the foundation of the educational project. For example, while color and relationships are explored with all students as part of the foundation at Pablo Neruda, the projects discussed in the *intento progettuale* include music and getting to know the incoming students. This is another element of the *progettazione:* hypotheses and areas of research the teachers would like to focus on in addition to the foundation. As the children spend more time in the school, the *intento progettuale* becomes more complex as the interests of the teacher as researcher are woven into the foundation created for the students.

Unlike in most American approaches to curriculum, the projects are not constructed in an effort to cover the curriculum. Whereas in the United States the curriculum is often created to meet standards, in Italy the foundational areas to explore are embedded in a project that is of interest to the children. This is what fuels the investigation, the asking and answering of questions, the development of critical thinking skills.

INTENTO PROGETTUALE OR INTENDED PROJECTS

There has been a great deal of discussion in the field of early childhood about the meetings that take place at the schools in Reggio Emilia to review the projects, listen to critical feedback from colleagues, and get a sense of what is happening in each of the classrooms. What follows is a translation of the first few pages of the *Intento Progettuale,* or intended projects, from 1998–1999. It is a research plan with ideas about what will be covered and a beginning analysis of the identity of the children as a group. This serves as the beginning of the voyage the teachers will take with their students over the next three years and will be revised, revisited, and fleshed out in weekly meetings with the entire school staff.

The most basic level includes the project themes for every child in every class at the school. These projects evolve over the course of three years. They may not be exactly the same for every class that comes through the school, as every teacher is different and may want to explore variations on themes. The main themes stay the same, however, since they tie into the things children have a right to explore and therefore create the foundation for the work in the schools of Reggio. Some examples from Scuola dell'Infanzia Pablo Neruda would be:

1. *Colore tra le mani:* a color theory project in which children use many different languages to explore and create their own understanding of color theory
2. *Segnalibro:* the first introduction to books, the structure of a book, reading, being read to, and storytelling
3. *Messaggi:* the exchange of messages that begin with symbols and progress to letters and finally written words
4. *Dare e darsi identità:* giving oneself and others identity

PROJECT THEMES	ENVIRONMENTAL PROJECTS	DAILY LIFE PROJECTS	SELF-MANAGED PROJECTS
Definition: This is the foundation, projects that all children will do in the course of three years.	**Definition:** These are projects that grow out of the classroom areas.	**Definition:** These are projects that spontaneously emerge during assembly or daily life at school.	**Definition:** These are projects set up for the children to do independently, alone or with a friend.
Examples: *Colore tra le mani:* Color among the Hands *Dare e darsi identità:* Giving Oneself and Others Identity *Processi di relazione:* Process of Relationships *Messaggi:* Messages *Segnalibro:* Bookmark *Compleanni:* Birthdays	**Examples:** Construction Light table Mirror triangle Messages Books Construction Dress up	**Examples:** Lunch Assembly Groupings *Stare a tavola* Arrival/departure Conflicts Outdoors	**Examples:** a metal sculpture project a weaving frame

5. *Processi di relazione:* developing, cultivating, and maintaining relationships with others

These projects can be the foundation on which many activities at the beginning of the year, are structured. These themes are explored in different ways and with different languages depending on the teacher's group of students.

The following excerpts of the *intento progettuale* are from the four-year-old class that began at Neruda the previous year. Their teachers created this when the students first arrived at the school; therefore, it was already a year old when I arrived. The excerpts have been edited for the purposes of our work. The first excerpt is from the teachers' notes based on their research to determine the main project themes for the three years the class will be attending Neruda.

The Premise—Section A
Teachers: Paola Ascari and Patrizia Margini

Within the net of *progettazione* we seek to make evident as much as possible the strategies of relationships (between teachers and parents, teachers and students, students and students) and the connection between the quality and the articulation of both time and context—in other words, "the things this time is made of."

For the purposes of writing, we will follow in a linear fashion the following core concepts, which are the basis of the first few months of school.

- The identity of the class
- The context of our research
- The hypothesis of development
- The strategies and instruments of observation and documentation

We are seeking to collect some moments that reveal the identity of the group, important points upon which we will begin to construct the project of the class. We have immediately begun to develop a space that could become "open," a space in which children are welcomed and that gives visibility to individual children as well as the group.

Meetings with the Families

These meetings took place in the month of July with only one teacher, Paola, because Patrizia was on maternity leave. The choice to have these meetings in July was linked to the intention to have time to reflect, elaborate, and synthesize the information gathered during these meetings. We proposed questions to the families related to the context of school experiences and to the hypothesis about things to explore in the first days of school:

- Strategies of *conquista,* or winning over
- Meeting literature
- Meeting music

Strategies of *Conquista*

At the end of the meetings with the families we asked, "If you were to suggest a way or a strategy to win over or enter a bit easily into a relationship with your child, what advice would you give?"

Read and re-tell
Pay attention to the child
Share common experiences
Give the child responsibilities
Play together
Listen to the child
Ask the child for help
Enter into dialogue with the child
Let the child follow his rhythm and time
Participate in the child's games
Let the child guide
Make the child feel important and considered

What follows is the first set of intended projects *(intento progettuale)* that Paola and Patrizia put forth for the beginning of the year with their new students.

Segnalibro (meeting literature)
Meeting music
Birth
Christmas

You can see that the *intento progettuale* is very fluid for the incoming students. Below is a summary of what Antonia created as her portion of the *intento progettuale* for the returning four-year-olds.

The Premise—Section B
Percorsi Grafici (Graphic Voyage—Drawing)
Communicare Tra Gli Amici (Communication between Friends)
I Compleanni (Birthdays)
Il Segnalibro (The Bookmark)
In Ascolto: Percorsi Musicali (Listening: Musical Voyage)

The *intento progettuale* becomes much more detailed the further along the students progress in school and includes hypotheses, strategies for research, strategies for observation, and experiences that continue from year to year. Essentially the *intento progettuale* is a map for the teachers, *atelierista,* and *pedagogista* to write, reflect, and share their work as it develops. The *intento progettuale* I have from 1998–1999 is eighty-three pages long.

As each group of students progresses through the school, the projects themselves also gain in complexity. For instance, let's take the *colore tra le mani* project and see how it might evolve through three years with one group of students. Periodically, meaning two or three times per academic year, the three-year-olds are invited to paint outdoors on easels. The children are observed while they paint to see if there are colors used commonly by the children or if there are subject matters that emerge frequently. At the end of the painting, when the children are satisfied with the work they have done, they are usually asked if they would like to name their paintings.

There are also appointments that children have within these projects that grow and evolve with the children during the course of three years. For example, color could be explored with watercolors, tempera, markers, colored pencils, oil paints, or liquid watercolors. These media could be used under the umbrella theme of color with projects that can include the exploration of shades of green found in springtime or the different reds and pinks of a table covered with rose petals. Each of these mini-projects is tied together by the same thread: *colore tra le mani.*

Appointments are events in which all children in a class will participate, and they may occur at any time. For instance, when the three-year-olds began at Neruda, they had an "appointment" to paint outside. This gave the teachers an opportunity to observe the way the students engaged the medium and the influence they had upon each other, as well as an opportunity to see if themes emerged. Within an ongoing project, not all students would necessarily participate in every initiative or language that was offered. An appointment, however, is a common experience within a larger body of work that all students would have in common. Another example would be the opportunity to go to the atelier and mix color, name the colors, and paint with them. All of the children did this several times over the course of the year, and it was a unifying activity within a larger *percorso,* or voyage. In addition, all of the students worked on self-portraits, although not necessarily on the same day. Within the students' collections of work created over the course of three years, there would be many commonalities and many things that small groups did, even though the body of work did not consist of the exact same experiences for all of the children in a class.

While I was at Neruda, Simonetta noticed that many children used the sea as one of the words in the titles of their paintings. This became the point of departure for a conversation with her class during their assembly in the subsequent days. The teachers paid attention and developed this thread into a project. The next step was to begin talking about it and listening to the children. They asked the children, "We noticed there are a lot of you who painted the sea." Then they waited a moment, even though it was silent—a thoughtful silence—and the children began speaking. This is the classic Reggio table-tennis way of conversing. Depending on what the teachers hear, they're off on a conversation. In this case, they explored all of the shades of blue, which were created by the children and then used to continue painting within the color project.

Here's another example. One day I was with Antonia and the five-year-olds, and the students were talking about shadows. We listened as they discussed how shadows move and whether or not they are connected to our bodies. Antonia asked the students, "If you are wearing bright yellow, will your shadow be yellow too?" There was a momentary pause, and then the students began responding, sharing their views. Some said yes; some said no; some reverted back to the earlier discussion. We listened, with Antonia trying to have the students speak individually so we could listen to them. Then Antonia synthesized what she heard and asked another question, "So, you are saying that while your shadow is a copy of you, it would not be colored?" Then the students re-constructed what they heard to clarify our understanding.

Another example of the ping-pong questioning is from an interaction I observed one day in the yard. Some students were playing, and one was offended by another. They came running to Antonia to tattle, and she listened and then asked, "What would you like me to do?" The students began to list the punishments they deemed appropriate for the crime. Antonia listened and repeated back to the students what she heard, punctuating the summary with another question. "So, you think. . . . Does that seem fair to you?" Again the students responded, and Antonia listened. Antonia has asked this kind of question on numerous occasions, and it provokes opinions and thinking from the students. Antonia and the other teachers then summarize and give back to the students what they have heard, sometimes with an additional question and sometimes not. The students are able to hear their own words and modify them as they see fit for clarity, constructing knowledge in the process.

I have also seen Antonia use this questioning strategy over an extended period of time. A new student arrived at Neruda in the third and final year at the school. Antonia had asked the students at the beginning how they might welcome Guido to the group, and they had offered a number of ways to do so. The conversation ended there, but Antonia picked it up again several months later, reminding the students, from her notes, of their words when the question had first been posed. Now, as she summarized their initial responses, she asked, "Is Guido what you expected?" She did not pepper them with many questions at a time but permitted the students to begin there, and then, still using her notes to drive the discussion, she framed the current questions around the earlier responses. This speaks both to the ping-pong questioning and the notion of wait time.

The four- and five-year-olds pick up where they left off at the end of the previous year. An example of this might be examining color more deeply with the four-year-olds than had been done the previous year when they were three. The teachers might have a painting "appointment" with the students similar to that used at the beginning of the previous year. The students would be invited to paint in the atelier or outdoors on easels and observed. The teachers might look for new patterns such as uses of color, student interaction, or influence that had not existed the year before. Or the teachers could take students to the atelier in small groups to mix paints and see what emerged, building upon what had occurred the year before. Another opportunity might be to engage the students in a discussion during the morning assembly and tape-record what the students had to say (to be transcribed later) about color. The teachers might ask, "What do we know about color?" The students would begin the project from this point, using their experiences from the previous year and any that may have occurred in the meantime to begin constructing the next chapter of their exploration of color.

Another example of an appointment within the color theme is the development of a color palette and observation of the ways students use the materials. All students are invited to the atelier to mix paint, and, depending upon what happens there or what emerges from the observations, the project can take on multiple directions in response to the interests of the children. For example, the students may have a theme emerge while naming the paints that takes on a life of its own as a project. Or the themes that come from the painting may lend themselves to a project. What matters most for our purposes here is that color has been established as one of the things children have a right to explore in Reggio Emilia. The manner in which it is explored will differ from group to group. From my understanding and my questioning of Mara, the *atelierista,* there are several things children are believed to have a right to explore: color, drawing, books, relationships. These may be the same or different at different schools and may manifest differently from year to year.

ENVIRONMENTAL PROJECTS

This type of project emerges directly from the space in which the children live and work. These projects are inherently built into the classroom as part of the space, including construction, house play, messages, books, games, and the light table. Project choices offered each day are drawn from these environmental sources as well. For example, the construction area and the house-play area are offered as choices on most days, and while the play in these spaces sustains the development of children independently, other projects may emerge from the teachers' observation of the way students use these spaces.

At the Nido, Lucia shared with me a project that emerged from her students' keen interest in dress up and play in characters. From there some parents built a theater to accommodate what was observed as an interest of the children. At Neruda, Paola and Patrizia began to note the way students sat together or sat alone during lunch. They began to look closely at who sat where and who sat alone. From there they offered students an opportunity to invite another classmate to dine at a separate table for two, in a room off of the lunchroom. They kept track of who was invited by whom, which revealed who was socially integrated and who was not. From there they drew a map of the lunchroom and took note of the places the children chose to sit each day for one month. This was all part of the use of the environment but provided valuable information about the development of the students individually and the composite of the class as a whole.

From these spaces, if a teacher is attentive, other projects can emerge, like one from house play, which deals with establishing identity, or a theater project based on children's make-believe that is observed by the teachers in the dress-up area.

The term *environmental projects* simply classifies part of the emergent work that is easily recognized as stemming from the environment. For instance, the children are interested in building in the construction area every day, so this is offered every day. The construction area also supports literacy development, as this is where students make up a lot of their stories. The kids also have the opportunity to leave their structures up for longer periods of time, work on them for more days, and narrate stories connected with what they build. In the dress-up and house-play area I watched a large group of children act out a birthday party, boys and girls together. This is a place to work out things from their home lives, build relationships, and tell stories; it is a popular choice every day. The house-play and dress-up area also offers many possibilities for symbolic play. If a teacher chooses to observe in the house-play area for a week or two, she will see patterns of who plays there and what types of games are played, real life or imaginary. The teacher can observe how the children use language—whether it is adult language or made-up language. Patterns will emerge over a short period of time, and then it is up to the teacher to pose a question to the students to find out what might lie beneath the choices they are making within their play. Depending on how the students respond, the teacher might make a proposal for a particular type of situation, player, or dress to see how the children take this on.

DAILY LIFE PROJECTS

The next category of projects are those that emerge from the day-to-day life lived with kids. These could be based on, for example, the children's response to work going on in the yard next door or to the yellow daisies they passed on the way to school in the car. These projects could go in any direction depending on what the children have observed and hypothesized. This is by far the most flexible category of projects and the most difficult to conceptualize. The day-to-day themes may be determined by the seasons, the weather, a conversation overheard in the bathroom, or patterns of play in the yard. It is a matter of looking at the moments that take place and listening to the children.

One day there was a bit of a discussion with Antonia and the five-year-olds about building and who wanted to go to the construction area. The children were not satisfied with the group Antonia chose because they had different building styles. One boy shared that he found his classmate disorganized and a bit messy. From here, Antonia asked all of the children at one point or another over the next couple of weeks to create a model of what they deemed to be disorder. She provided materials—craft sticks and some little round pebbles—and asked the students to create an image of disorder. This provided a rich context to discuss order and disorder with the entire group and examine how different each of their definitions could be. The conversation Antonia had in the outdoors regarding punishing a student for an unseen offense also became a project in the same way. Here is where things spiral back one onto another, because this latter example fell within the foundational project called "Process of Relationships," although it originally stemmed from day-to-day life. This is an example of how difficult it is to separate the Reggio approach into categories.

SELF-MANAGED PROJECTS

Finally, self-managed projects are offered concurrently for small periods of time alongside the other types of projects I have already discussed. When I arrived at Neruda, one of the choices offered the children was large metal sculptures. These had been begun in an effort to inhabit the classroom into which they had just moved. Next to a large tangle of wire about 2 by 2 feet stood a container full of different pieces of metal wire, copper, foil, and blue fabric. The children were invited to tie these little pieces to the large tangle. These eventually became "clouds" according to the children. It was available for the children to work on before school, while waiting for parents after school, and during project time. Another example of a self-managed project would be a weave: a simple project in which a frame is set up and offered at different times during the day.

Self-managed projects offered periodic opportunities for the children to float to and away from an activity. This is the environment as the third teacher, supporting the interaction and learning of the students without direct adult intervention. These self-managed projects also provided places for children to socialize, to chat, and to be together quietly with friends while their hands were active.

Reflecting on Your Curriculum

Looking again at your vision, take a moment and choose three things that you believe young children have a right to explore from the list you created at the beginning of this chapter. It is important that these are aligned with what has been stated in chapter 1, so take a moment to think about it carefully. While it is possible to borrow from the schools of Reggio here, as they have identified some of the larger themes in a young child's life, choose what works for you and your setting. Relationships are important, and so is communication. Art, be it color, drawing, or self-expression, is also fruitful in the lives of children. Remember that it is too much to try and put all of this into a school in one year. Choose three themes to begin creating a foundation that is in keeping with your vision and will complement both your environment and your use of time. As you begin to work within this structure, you will notice that some projects fall into more than one category. That is to be expected; it is this way in Reggio too. But three fundamental concepts, coupled with daily life at school and what is offered through the environment, will be more than enough to gain insight into working in a way similar to *progettazione*. As well, this process of choosing, hypothesizing, and testing encompasses another key component of *progettazione*—the teacher as researcher working parallel to her students.

- What do children have a right to explore? What is fundamental to being human?
- What could you offer children over the course of three years that could become a part of your school?
- What base projects might work in your school?
- What types of environmental projects might be supported by your workspace?
- What ideas of self-managed projects might work at your site?

Progettazione at Your School

Now that we have examined the ideas of *progettazione* and *intento progettuale,* along with a number of examples, let's break the *percorso* or voyage of a project into smaller components, which will be useful in implementing the answers provided above. Here are the parts of project work I observed, which we'll talk about next:

- Beginning a Project: Asking Questions and Wait Time
- Developing the Project Idea
- Carrying Out the Project
- Documenting the Project

BEGINNING A PROJECT: ASKING QUESTIONS AND WAIT TIME

Projects can begin by listening to children talk, taking notes or tape-recording the conversation, and repeating back to the kids what you hear them saying. Projects can also begin by your posing a question that has occurred to you through your observations of the classroom and the children or in order to open a discussion of one of the foundational concepts you intend to explore with your students.

Once the question has been posed, the issue becomes how long to wait before raising the topic again or supplying a new *provocazione.* In Reggio, teachers often wait much longer than seems bearable to American teachers. We are going to look at both skills—asking questions and waiting—in this section.

Questions

When opening a conversation that may lead to a project, teachers in Reggio often begin with an observation they have made or an honest question.

For example, after the children gathered daisies, teachers asked them questions like, "What do you notice about the shape of the flowers?" This was the birth of a project on shape and symmetry. These can also be questions the teachers had prepared ahead of time. Paola and Patrizia did a project for the birthdays of the students, and asked the children as their birthdays approached, "Do you remember where you were before you were born?" One child responded, "I waited for my mother to call me." The children were asked to represent their answers visually, and this became a beautiful project. For the opening of the project *Il Segnalibro,* the children were asked, "Do three-year-old children read?" The students had opinions about this and brought books to school to demonstrate their ability to read. In reality they knew the stories so well they simply retold them page by page as they remembered the stories being told to them.

Once the conversation is moving along, teachers continue to use open-ended questions that begin with "how": How would you do that? How could that be done? Or "what": What might we want to do? What makes that a good idea? This gets the children formulating and expressing their own hypotheses and opinions.

The educators I worked with in Reggio Emilia avoided questions that begin with "why." "Why" is a difficult question, conceptually, for young children. In many cases teachers in the United States push for "why," which in reality does not matter nor affect the project to any great degree. I encourage teachers to use concrete questions that are easily answered. "How" and "what" are accessible to young children. They can tell you how to do something or what it is or means. This is not to say there is not a place for questions of "why," but I encourage teachers not to rely on "why" as a pivotal question, as it often leaves children without an answer.

In the beginning it will be easier to write questions out to pose to the children in an effort to develop the habit of ping-ponging and listening. Then the questions will begin to come on their own throughout the day. Instead of asking multiple questions at the same time, teachers in Reggio tend to ask one thoughtful question that can be synthesized or left to pick up another day.

In Reggio, teachers are often groomed not to answer the questions the children pose. Paola told me, "Never directly answer a child's question, but ask them what they think first." If a child has a question, she more than likely has a hypothesis as well. When you encourage children to state these opinions, you are able to build upon their hypothesis or help them break it down. This is good practice on many levels, but it is also often contrary to the ways in which we have been trained and our knee-jerk reaction to a question posed to us by a child—to give them the answer as we understand it. Instead we can help them find or express their own answers. Isn't this one of the roles of education—equipping children to ask and answer their own questions, giving them the skills and tools to continue asking and answering the questions that frame our lives?

The Brazilian educator and author Paulo Freire talks about a drive-through education in which, when children ask us something, we hand them neatly packaged answers that fit our understanding of both the question and what we think they need to know as the answer. In both Freire's view and the Reggio view, such an education is not education at all. If we believe that learning is building, de-construction, and ultimately re-building knowledge over time, handing the child or the learner a correct answer, while perhaps easier in the moment, does not aid in this process. Carlina Rinaldi (1994) makes a point that cannot be over-emphasized:

> If we believe children possess their own theories, interpretations and questions, and are the co-protagonists in the knowledge building processes, then the most important verb in the educational practice is no longer to TALK, to EXPLAIN or to TRANSMIT . . . but to LISTEN. Listening is the availability to others and what they have to say, listening to the hundred plus languages with all the senses. To listen is a reciprocal verb. Listening legitimizes the other person because communication is one of the fundamental means of giving form to thought.

Here's an example of the conversation that began a project on numbers in the four-year-old class at Pablo Neruda. Paola, one of the teachers of the four-year-olds, finished talking to a parent and joined the rest of the group for assembly.

"Okay, okay," began Paola, and the children quieted down, eating their fruit and waiting. "Yesterday, Davide's mother asked me an interesting question, and I wanted to ask you the same question." As she said this, the children leaned forward to hear this interesting question. Paola continued, "Davide learned to count to five from Donald Duck, and his mom wants to know, and so do I, should a child of four years old know the numbers, and how can they be learned and what do they serve?"

There was a brief moment of silence, and then like firecrackers the children began to offer their experiences and opinions about counting. As the children talked, Patrizia slipped away to get some paper and write down their words, while Paola managed the discussion.

Giorgia shared her ability to count, "One, two, three, four . . ." Francesca joined Giorgia, and they progressed to twenty.

Caterina added, "There are numbers everywhere—calendars, books . . . You can see them all around you."

Paola took Caterina's words and re-launched what she heard. "Okay, if there are numbers everywhere, tell me, where else do you see numbers?"

The children scrambled to offer their ideas to the conversation.

"In the supermarket . . . at the bus stop . . . television . . . the newspaper . . ." In a rush of voices Simone, Fabio, and Francesco contributed. Paola listened, Patrizia wrote, and Paola re-launched again.

"Okay, so there are numbers everywhere. Is this useful? How is this useful?"

Caterina assured Paola that it is useful and important information and in fact she can count to thirty, and she began to demonstrate. Giorgia and Francesca agreed with Caterina and began to suggest purposes for numbers, and the conversation was off and running.

The story illustrates the way in which the *reggiani* articulate their values and view of the child as protagonist and then behave in the same way. The vision is aligned with the practice. The students are put in the center of the conversation in order to reason through and arrive at the appropriate responses for them. Notice that it is not a matter of children coming to the "right" answer but rather the appropriate answer that may very well be factually erroneous. It is the process the children go through that carries the lessons.

Wait Time

After listening to the children, Reggio teachers reflect back what they hear children say and leave it to simmer with them a bit. That can be for the hour, the day, or the week—there is no formula for the right amount of time. Sometimes the children then re-broach the subject with a teacher. This might happen in small groups, with individuals, or with the whole class in a morning meeting. Whether or not that happens, teachers might bring it up again in a small or large group setting—when playing outside with a few kids, for example, or in the mini-atelier with a small group that is being tape-recorded. This is where the children demonstrate time after time that they have thoughtfully considered the topic in a variety of settings and have made connections on their own. Having done so, they are ready to share their thoughts with the teacher and the class, in their own time.

In Reggio, when I was trying to come to terms with the idea of wait time, I was told to wait past the moment of comfort for me. Wait time can extend for hours or even days from one conversation to the next on any particular subject. In my first project (see below), on deciding how to change the space that the four-year-olds would move into as five-year-olds, Patrizia and Paola opened the conversation and then left the ideas to germinate for more than one day between conversations. There was not the notion that these conversations and events needed to happen in a linear, day-after-day way, like checking things off of a neat list.

Patrizia told me that students make connection in their own time and in all sorts of places. If we are talking about plants, for instance, some students would reflect on it that day after school, or even in that moment, while others would make their connections in a longer period of time. If the follow-up conversation took place too soon, some students would be excluded. If we think that part of learning is about making connections, then it is difficult to mandate or manage the time in which these connections take place in the minds of individuals. We each operate on a different timeline. Children also make connections in their own time, and this time needs to be respected.

DEVELOPING THE PROJECT IDEA

It is impossible to give you instructions for a format at this point, because it then becomes static and not responsive to the individual group of children and the unique situation of your program. Instead you will be working in ways that are based on inquiry for yourself and your students. Therefore, try something, take notes for yourself, modify it, and try again.

In Reggio, questions are asked and the conversations developed over the course of time—certainly more than one day. The questioning might be followed by a trip somewhere else in the school to look at a space or an object related to the discussion. For example, when we talked to the students about beginning to inhabit the five-year-old classroom and creating something for the space, we initially had a short conversation on the topic in morning assembly. Then a day or so later, we took the class there to look it over and then let them think about it for a couple of days. When Simonetta and the three-year-olds began talking about color, she took the students to the atelier to look at all of the different colored paints and the work of other students on the easels before asking the question, "What is color?" When Paola and Patrizia wanted to begin examining shape and symmetry, they took the students outside to gather flowers before beginning any discussion at all. I have seen Antonia bring work of former students to her class and get responses from her students about what they thought, without guiding their reactions. The students responded freely while she took notes, and then she synthesized what she heard on another day to begin the discussion about equilibrium. Antonia also had older brothers and sisters of students come to class to talk about elementary school as a way of opening a discussion and project on the transition her students would make the next year. A project can emerge in many, many forms from a direct question to an observation, a *provocazione,* discussion in small or large group, and many others.

CARRYING OUT THE PROJECT

Once the idea for a project is established, one must begin to ask all of the questions necessary to plan and execute the project. This is where I have heard teachers in the United States talk about "webbing." I have never seen any type of webbing, per se, in my time in Reggio. Instead, the who, what, when, where, why, and how questions are asked to flesh out all of the details and establish parameters for the project.

Whatever materials or arrangements of personnel may be involved, this is the time to engage in that part of the project preparation. This is a more complex part than it seems. There are always many essential details you have not thought of. I remember when I worked on my first project alone and thought I was ready, having prepared the day before. But I had chosen the wrong size of paint brushes, and the liquid watercolors were not diluted enough, so I was trying to make the necessary changes while managing the kids. It was not as I had anticipated, but from that experience I learned the necessity of thorough preparation so that I can be fully present when the students arrive.

The project itself may involve any of the "hundred languages"—for example, painting, papier-mâché, clay, music recordings, playacting, work on the computer—or it could involve exploration of a topic such as "the city" through as many as seven or eight languages all within the same project.

DOCUMENTING THE PROJECT

The documentation of a project is vitally important not only for the students but also for your professional development as a teacher. Documenting the project allows the children to look at their own work and be reminded of their thinking. It allows you to reflect upon what is actually happening with the children and perhaps see a new direction emerge or see the need for different resources. Documentation makes processes visible—both the teachers' and the children's. Documentation also gives you the opportunity to make the process visible and share elements of your time with the children that otherwise would be missed by the families. The parents are able to see not only what their children have done at school but also how it was done and who participated.

Documentation can take many forms, but some tools should be on hand; for example, a camera, whether 35 mm, digital, or disposable; a tape recorder with blank tapes; a video camera; something to write with, such as a pad of paper and a pen, for observations and drawings. Not all types of documentation will be used on all projects, but having the materials available creates possibilities for the teachers and the students. Look for opportunities to photograph groups of children while working on the project, to make audio recordings of the conversations involved in the planning of the project, and to record written observations of the children at all stages of project development. The idea is twofold: to make visible the children's process as it unfolds and to make visible the teachers' process to share and learn from. As the project occurs, collect artifacts to review and reflect upon at a later time. The next chapter will talk about the process of documentation in more detail.

Walking through a Sample Project

In order to show the possibilities for a project with children, here is a discussion of my first project in Reggio, at Pablo Neruda. It began with a discussion with the four-year-olds about their coming move to the five-year-old classroom.

Original transcript of the conversation in Italian:

Patrizia: *Dall'inizio dell'anno ad adesso la nostra sezione si è trasformata. Tra pochi giorni, dopo le vacanze dell'estate, noi andremo su nella sezione dei 5 anni . . .*

Francesco: *questa scuola è un grandissimo palazzo!*
Patrizia: *Io, Julie e Paola siamo andate su ieri per vedere la nuova sezione e capire se potevamo già iniziare a preparare qualcosa di bello . . . passando dalla torretta abbiamo notato che c'è molto spazio in verticale. È cioè altissimo e vuoto . . .*
Giorgia: *noi possiamo ricrearlo!*
Patrizia: *Come?*
Giorgia: *possiamo metterci delle cose che ci piacciono di più!*

Here is the conversation translated into English:

Patrizia: From the beginning of the year to now, our classroom has been transformed. In just a few days, after the summer vacation, we'll go up into the five-year-old classroom. . . .
Francesco: . . . This school is a giant building!
Patrizia: Julie, Paola, and I went upstairs yesterday to see the classroom and to see if we could already start to make something beautiful. . . . Passing through the tower, we noticed that there is a lot of vertical space. It is really high and empty. . . .
Giorgia: We can re-create it!
Patrizia: How?
Giorgia: We can put things there that we like better. . . .

And so the project began with the proposal of a space to fill. After this initial conversation, we waited a day, and then we went to the next level of defining the project. This involved taking small groups of children upstairs to look around at the section and, in particular, to visit the tower and see what it suggested to the children. The children proposed a number of things. The one that suited the space the best and that the students were most excited about was the idea of creating a fresco that would hang vertically to fill the space. This project would serve to facilitate the concept of continuity and change by helping the students begin inhabiting their new space.

Once the students seemed decided on the idea of a fresco, we asked the children to think about what kind of subject matter might lend itself to the space. The question was left to simmer for a few days. Then, during the assembly, the subject of the fresco was raised, and at this point Patty and I took a small group of children, who had expressed a keen interest in this project, into the mini-atelier to discuss it. Afterwards, we took this group upstairs to visit the space again and brainstorm together about what kind of painting might lend itself to the space. One girl, Giorgia, suggested the sky during the conversation, and the students debated before finally agreeing with this choice.

Patty and Paola indicated that the materials for the artwork and the documentation would need to be prepared a day before beginning the project. They thought liquid watercolors would work best because of the subject matter and large dimensions of the art, which was projected to be about $2\frac{1}{2}$ to 3 meters in length. Preparations involved a lot of details, including obtaining many jars of paint, diluted or mixed to create different shades, collecting and cleaning brushes, and setting up the paper in the atelier so the students could go in and begin working right away. The cassette in the tape recorder needed to be rewound and ready to record the students while they worked. The digital camera needed to be charged and cleared of photos. The next day, during the assembly, the fresco was offered as one of the project choices along with three or four other things. Three students chose to participate, and the group went upstairs to begin. While the students were working, asking for help, or talking, the process was photographed and tape-recorded. This took place for several days until the fresco was completed. Then the tape was transcribed, and the photos were printed, which took several hours.

In discussing this rather short project with Paola and Patty afterwards, I found that I was not really able to share with them what I had learned about the children and their processes, because I had been so caught up in my own difficulties in facilitating the process. The documentation and artifacts proved to be simple and did not reveal much about the students or the way in which they worked. Instead, the artifacts revealed how limited my understanding and execution of *progettazione* truly was. Ultimately what I was able to document was my struggle with beginning to work in Reggio-inspired ways. The documentation of this *progettazione* was informative in ways we had not anticipated, as often occurs.

Thinking about Projects in Your Program

With the discussion in this chapter as your framework, and using the list of project concepts you wrote down, take a minute to respond to the following questions that will further shape your program. These are questions for a teacher to use in looking at a program. Depending on what happens as the project proceeds, conversations may follow to engage the children in exploring aspects of potential projects—why the space under the stairs is so inviting, for instance. As you think about these categories of projects, ask yourself how the three foundational concepts you chose earlier interact with any of these categories.

ENVIRONMENTAL PROJECTS

To think about what projects your environment might offer, ask yourself questions like these:

- What are the favorite parts of your school, where you often find groups of children? Where do children congregate?
- Are the groups in different high-use areas mostly boys, mostly girls, or balanced in terms of gender?
- How do the children play outdoors? Are there organized games, or do they organize themselves?
- What types of toys and make-believe games do children engage in?
- Do children use loud or soft voices?
- What kinds of things do students build?
- Do they use other toys to inhabit their structures?

DAILY LIFE PROJECTS

As you begin to think about creating projects from children's daily lives in the program, observe their relationships with one another. Ask yourself questions like these:

- Do the children greet each other easily?
- Are there cliques? How are students included or excluded from play?
- When are the easiest and most difficult transitions?
- Do the students want to play indoors or outdoors?
- Does the group have daily jokes or habits?

SELF-MANAGED PROJECTS

To come up with good self-managed projects to have available to students in your classroom, consider questions like these:

- What does the space offer? For example, there may be a chain-link fence around the playground that could be used for weaving.
- Could the students create artifacts to inhabit the space?
- Could the students help prepare materials to have on hand for other offerings? For example, perhaps they could tear strips of paper for papier-mâché or cut out pictures to be used in "messages."

By taking notes for yourself on the topics above, you can develop ideas to propose to the students. Depending on their responses, or lack thereof, a project may emerge that you would not have anticipated. Having this observable information available and forming questions ahead of time will make launching a project much clearer.

As a hypothetical example, let's continue with the space under the stairs. Imagine you have an empty space under the stairs with cushions and a curtain for privacy. You have noticed the children love it, and there are always two or three children there. You might ask the group, "What is it about under the stairs that is so inviting? What do you do under the stairs that you cannot do in the classroom?" Then listen to the students, and take notes or tape-record the exchange to listen to again later. Suppose the students share that they can have quiet time with friends for secrets and reading books. You might ask, "Is there anywhere else that those things might take place?" The students might share places at school or away from school where they get the same feeling.

This first portion is the birth of the project. From here you can focus your discussions on defining what can occur in a space like this; have the students describe and define it for you. You might bring in magazines for students to choose pictures of other spaces that are appealing. This is where you are developing the project. The project might entail creating more special places like this around the school, or it might simply be a study of what makes this space so special. It would depend on the response of the students. The enthusiasm of the students must determine the evolution of the work. A project may seem potentially fabulous to us, but not catch fire with the students, in which case there is no reason to force it.

It will help in making children's interests visible if you can commit to observing students in one section of the school every day for thirty minutes. It could be at the same time or different times of day to see how the area is used. For example, you could set up paint easels and offer these as a project choice. Make note of who wants to paint, how many days a week they want to paint, and how long they stay at the easel. Do the children talk to each other while painting? Do they give each other feedback on their work?

Another powerful exercise is to begin each day with a class meeting and give yourself the freedom to engage the students fully by tape-recording the conversation. Then transcribe the tape before going home, and at the end of two weeks look over the transcriptions, looking for patterns. How are the children participating? Are some children silent while others dominate? Do they discuss the topic at hand or tangential topics? What topics recur?

This is an opportunity to gather information about your students while developing yourself professionally. It is a time commitment, especially the transcriptions, but it is time well spent. From this raw data about your students, you will be able to drive your intended projects with valuable information about your students and their interests. You might discover communication habits worth exploring or interesting ways of relating that would fit perfectly into one of your three chosen categories. Also, patterns about the daily life of your school or the way students live in the environment may reveal themselves. From this information you can hypothesize and bring it back to your students. Here are some examples of statements drawn from classroom observations and questions to jump-start conversations about them:

- "I noticed that during the morning meeting (only five students talked, students brought toys to the meeting, some sat on chairs while others on the floor). Can you tell me how or why this happens?"
- "When I observed the library area, many of you were (reading to each other, mimicking adults). Could you tell me more about this?"
- "While playing outside I saw (make-believe gun play, kung fu, tag with rules understood by the students). Can you tell me more about this game?"

In your notebook, take a minute to write down a few questions that you might ask to begin talking to students about one of your project ideas.

Teachers—like children and everyone else—feel the need to grow in their competences; they want to transform experiences into thoughts, thoughts into reflections, and reflections into new thoughts and new actions. They also feel a need to make predictions, to try things out, and to interpret them. . . . Teachers must learn to interpret ongoing processes rather than wait to evaluate results.

—LORIS MALAGUZZI

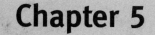

Chapter 5

Observation and Documentation

One of the international trademarks of the Reggio approach to education is the way that Reggio schools document the process of the students' and teachers' work. What the schools of Reggio Emilia have done with documentation is the most innovative look at making learning visible. By documenting our work we create a powerful legacy of work to be viewed and a powerful tool for our own professional development. The concept of making the learning visible carries with it a number of audiences. It is not simply a matter of photographing the students while they are involved in a particular activity; it is collecting their work and experiences in as many media as possible and then looking at these to see what emerges for the benefit of all the adults and children involved.

What Is Documentation?

The words of Carlina Rinaldi (1994) on the Reggio perspective on documentation will serve to frame our discussion:

> Documentation is the process of gathering evidence and artifacts of what happens in the classroom. Documentation is not only the *process* of gathering evidence and artifacts, but also a physical *collection* of evidence and artifacts, the *reflection* on and analysis of the collection, and the presentation of that collection, or part of it, in a way that makes children's learning visible to the children, to the teachers, to other adults including families and visitors (i.e. documentation panels, videos, artifacts and products produced by children with accompanying observations or slide shows of the process).

Documentation begins from observation. Observations can be handwritten, tape-recorded, or videotaped. The observations can become part of a larger documentation, or they can be considered documentation on their own. But we can deduce from the words of Carlina Rinaldi that observation is the beginning of almost all documentation. It is important to note that documentation and documentation panels are different. Documentation is a part of the process of *progettazione,* while the panels are the product of the process of documentation. Documentation is a process itself, a part of *progettazione* but substantive enough to merit a deep exploration as a tool for the entire school community.

What can be documented? This question is difficult to answer without limiting the possibilities. You can document the processes of both the teachers and the students. Over time, the most common documentation I have seen is of the chronological process of what actually happened within a course of work. This is just the beginning and serves as almost the most basic form of documentation. This may be a good way for you to start; as you reflect on the seemingly linear process, laid out step by step, other themes will emerge. Documentation can serve to illuminate the thinking, a change in thinking that occurred, what was learned or not learned, the evolution of behavior, questioning, maturity, responses, and opinions. For example, while I was with Paola and Patty's class of four-year-olds, the children worked on self-portraits. This work was tied to the larger themes of self-identity and the exploration of graphics. While working with the students on rendering their own self-images, Paola and Patty offered students the opportunity to pose for one another, similar to the models that might be used in an art class. While some students volunteered to stand before their classmates and be drawn as soon as the opportunity was presented, others never indicated an inclination to do so. The teachers used this opportunity to examine and take note of who modeled and how they did so, posing and primping or in a relaxed, casual manner. These notes were also documentation of the project of the self-portraits—another opportunity to look at the evolution of the students' development of self-identity, buried within a project that seemed focused on something totally different.

Another example occurred while I was working at Nido Bellelli. Lucia was interested in how very young children encountered the computer as one of the "hundred languages." Children were invited to create scenes on the computer using a program that offered different backgrounds, animals, and so forth. While an obvious thread for documentation would be what was created and how the students did so, I was intrigued to see that Lucia focused on how the students "met" the computer. For most of the children this was their first chance to manipulate a computer, and their gusto or reservation, not what was produced, was what she noted. There are many ways to look at and think about all of the activities that occur within the work with young children. It is important sometimes to look beyond the obvious and peel back the layers of an experience to look at the children's development from another perspective. Every activity offers multiple possibilities for observing a facet of the children and their development. Therefore, open your mind to paying attention to something beyond the first or most obvious layer.

For example, you might observe the way students influence one another in particular situations, parts of the classroom, or diverse groupings.

The Foundation of Documentation: Observation

I refer again to the words of Carlina Rinaldi (1994) to frame our discussion of documentation:

> Observation and documentation are other key concepts of our approach. The theoretical premise is that there is no objective point of view that can make observation neutral. Point of view is always subjective, and observation always involves participation. But this is a strength, not a limitation. Subjectivity often frightens us, because it also means assuming responsibility. So the search for objectivity is often driven by the fear of responsibility. There is no existing objective adult point of view with respect to the child. Instead we have multiple interacting subjects who construct reality starting from different points of view, because observing means not so much perceiving reality as constructing reality.
>
> I observe you, and while I observe you, I "capture" you, I interpret you. But at the same time I also modify my own knowledge. So observation is not only an individual action but also a reciprocal relationship. It is an action, a relationship, a process that makes us aware of what is happening around us.

To observe is above all to choose, and so it is indispensable to make the field of observation limitless. Deciding what to observe is primarily the responsibility of the observer, but it is even better when the choice is shared by the group. In any case, the motivation that led to that observation must be clear. In addition to being a process, observation is in itself already an interpretation. What I observe is already a possible indication, which may confirm or refute my theories or hypotheses. Or my documentation may reveal something I never anticipated.

For instance, when Paola and Patty offered students the opportunity to invite another student to lunch, we were primarily looking at the development of relationships. However, the process also revealed a great deal about the social and emotional development of the students involved. Giorgia was invited to lunch with other students many times, while Enrico was not and had difficulty choosing a student with whom he wanted to have lunch. Enrico actually had difficulty remembering the names of all of his classmates. This was totally unanticipated, and of course we noted it and it informed our work with him. This example is discussed in more detail in the coming pages.

In my current work in education, the one thing from the schools of Reggio Emilia that resonates almost daily is how a teacher's practice changes most quickly and profoundly when she begins to observe children daily. For purposes of clarity I will use the term *observation* to mean watching and writing down the actions of the children at your school. This can be done in many different settings, including the lunchroom, outside, the classroom, and with a lot of different student groupings. It can be observing individual students working with a particular material, small groups working together, or all students in the play yard or lunchroom. This is the first and most powerful step towards changing your practice. Observation provides a way to look at the development of students in all domains, as well as an opportunity to create a window for parents to peer inside the daily life of the school and their children's activities there. These are often called *anecdotal records,* so that may be the term you are more accustomed to hearing.

Ahead you will look at the following:

- Where can you observe?
- What do you look for?
- How are observations structured?
- What can you do with observations when they are done?

After I had been working at Pablo Neruda for a number of months, Simonetta, one of the teachers of the three-year-olds, said she thought perhaps it was time for me to start observing students formally. I was not quite sure what she meant; I had been taking notes on my own since I had arrived at the school. Simonetta suggested that I go to the construction area and just watch the kids. I thought maybe she was just trying to get me out from underfoot, but I followed her instructions. I sat in the construction area with my notebook and pencil, and I observed. I had no idea what I was looking for. There had been no concrete instructions other than to watch what the children were doing. So, sitting with my back against the wall, I watched the three-year-olds who were building and using small plastic animals to create stories and inhabit their structures.

The next day, two of the three children from the first day came to the construction area and engaged me in a bit of conversation about their construction. They were building a castle, with the animals as the inhabitants. This theme had been present in their class since the previous year, so I tried to facilitate their exploration a little. On the third day I brought up a few books about castles that I found in the classroom; they included pictures of actual and imagined castles. The children consulted them and began to use these to aid in the construction. I made an effort to record as much as I could in a narrative, paragraph format.

After a few more days, Simonetta asked me to show her my observations. I produced a small pile of hastily written observations, and Simonetta took them in her hands, sat down, and quietly flipped through the pages. I waited for her feedback, and she began gently and concretely by asking me questions about the time frame in which these events took place.

"Julie, how much time passed in the construction area this morning?" she asked. I couldn't remember, and it was there that my real understanding of observation began. I was fortunate to have Simonetta to explain the finer points of watching children and recording what actually happened in their work and world. The most important point Simonetta made was that it was essential to capture what actually happened without trying to analyze it as it was happening. A well-done observation will contain all the information needed to keep it open for analysis and interpretation in the future, without interpreting any of what happens in the moment.

After our first conversation, Simonetta shared with me a format for observing one, two, or several students that was easy to replicate. My observations changed from a narrative to a spreadsheet of sorts, which shows the passage of time and the actions of children either simultaneously or consecutively. This observation tool for one child is reproduced on the following page. (A version for observing multiple children appears on p. 121.) With just a few modifications, it can be tailored for any setting. The left-hand column is used to record the time in minutes (a watch is handy!), while the right-hand columns record what is actually happening. Each time you write an observation in the right-hand column, there should be a time recorded. If you are observing more than one child interacting, you would have a column for each of them. This way you can see what each child said or did in relation to

Observation Tool		
Date:	Context:	Child:
Time		

©2005 Julianne Wurm. May be reproduced for use by teachers only.

OBSERVATION AND DOCUMENTATION   **103**

what other children are saying or doing, and also look at each child's column alone. When children's actions happen simultaneously, write them next to each other in their respective columns. When they happen a little before or after each other, write them a little farther up or down on the page, across from the appropriate time. Thus the sheet becomes a visual indicator of the cildren's actions in the passage of time.

On the next page is an example of an observation I completed in an American preschool using this form. In this observation from the summer of 2001, one can still see the events happening. Paired with photos of the child involved, this observation would be a useful tool for the teachers while at the same time a priceless piece of their child's day for the parents.

Antonia made another useful suggestion about observing and documenting the play of students. She encouraged me to observe children outside by choosing a place to watch and record what happened in that space rather than following the work of a specific child or group of children. This proved to be an interesting way to track both the way in which the children were using the outdoor space and the types of games they were playing. Children's outdoor play is often ignored in observing their work, and yet it is an important part of the "hundred languages" of children.

Making Observation an Everyday Practice

I realize it requires time to observe every day. It can seem like a luxury or an impossibility to remove yourself from the activity enough just to watch and take notes on what you see. However, this is probably the most powerful and immediate way to change your practice. Daily observation will reveal a wealth of information about students, about their development, and about your own work as a teacher. Only by practicing the activity of observation can you begin to critique your own ability to observe, document, and engage in *progettazione* with your students.

The simplest way to begin may be to choose a time of day or area of the classroom to observe for a week or two or even three. It was not by accident that Simonetta stationed me in one area of the classroom to begin my work of observation. The process of observing will in itself refine the practice. Another possibility is to begin by observing each other once or twice a week and then sharing these observations at a

Sample Observation

Date: *March 3, 2003*   **Context:** *finger painting alone*   **Child:** *Lucia*

Time	
1:55	*Using her right hand smearing paint on paper*
	Pushing it around
	Hesitant to use her left hand
1:58	*Puts paint on left hand*
	Rubbing hands (like washing)
	Chatters / laughs
	Rubbing hands
2:00	*Claps*
	Smearing in sweeping motions
	Looks at hands
	Right index finger traces left hand
2:01	*Smears on face*
	Puts hands in paint
	"Ooooooooh"s

meeting. The most important point to remember is to simply observe, not judge or interpret. This strategy has been successful for many teachers and might be a good place to start in order to develop observation skills and make observation a regular habit.

Why Document Children's Work?

Lucia, one of the teachers at Nido Bellelli, told me that a little child only discovers the world above her once. That is a marvelous day to witness, when the nine-month-old baby looks up and, with wonder, spends much of her day looking at the world above her that before this she was not fully aware of. Capturing that experience with a series of photos and a short observation creates a memorable glimpse of the child's daily life. In itself this documentation gives the teacher new insight into that child, insight that can be shared with the child's parents and used to concoct other experiences for that child.

Now, imagine that you were able to capture this moment in the lives of ten children. Looking at the observations and photos side by side, you might see that expressions of emotion at this event were similar, or that the surprise of discovering the world above was both delightful and frightening, or that the children made this discovery in quite different ways. These discoveries can only be made by documenting the experiences as they unfold over and over. For teachers who are also researchers, documentation is essential, because it provides the data on which their research is founded. Documentation can reveal subtle patterns about our students and refine our craft as professionals.

Carlina Rinaldi (1994) says about the role of documentation in the Reggio programs, "The role of the teacher also involves hypothesizing on the possible developments of the educational project and this is closely related to the other aspects that characterize the teacher's work: LISTENING, OBSERVATION, DOCUMENTATION and INTERPRETATION." Observation is listening with your eyes just like touching is a way of knowing something by using your fingers. By documenting students' work we are in essence documenting our own development as practitioners. Documentation offers vital information to teachers about themselves and their students, and it brings families "inside the story" of their children's lives at schools and can create a testimony of work done with children as it is collected over time.

THE USES OF DOCUMENTATION

It is impossible to provide a comprehensive list of options for documentation. Whatever method is used, it should serve to inform the protagonists of the experience (teachers, parents, and students). Here are some of the ways that documentation is used in the Reggio schools:

- For children to reflect on their own work
- For children to connect to and reflect on other children's work
- For adults to reflect on children's work and hypothesize about where their work with students might go next
- For families to experience the work and explorations of their children
- To document children's growth over time
- To develop a complex and detailed picture of the child in all developmental domains
- To provide a resource for the wider community of educators to understand children's learning better
- To share with a funder or the community at large what is happening inside a school

I have seen small children marvel at a documentation panel placed 10 inches off the floor on a wall, specifically for them. This documentation included both pictures and words: large (8 x 10 inches) black-and-white photographs of infants interacting with musical instruments and a small amount of text to create a context for the adults who enjoyed this with their children. The children were drawn to this part of the classroom. The students were intrigued by the photos of themselves and each other, and the vivid representation of emotion on the faces of the children was engaging. I saw infants mimic the smile of joy demonstrated by another child while shaking a homemade instrument filled with beans. I also saw a number of parents on the floor examining the photos and interacting with their children, with the documentation serving as an intermediary for this encounter. The placement and content of a piece of documentation can thus invite students and families to interact with the process of *progettazione*.

In the middle of a shopping mall in Reggio there was a 5-feet-high triangular documentation panel. Each of the three walls displayed photos, diagrams, and other content regarding the reconceptualization of a local school yard, which was like a park. Adults and children would stop, look, and point to different parts of the exhibit, talking about the project taking place. Not all of those who engaged this particular example of documentation were parents of young children, but they were part of the community at large and took an interest in life inside the local schools. This example demonstrates the use of documentation to inform and engage the community. Documentation can also be used by professionals to reflect upon their own work; by parents to get inside the day-to-day experience and cognitive, social, emotional, or physical development of their children; to communicate to the families, community, or larger educational community surrounding the schools; and to reflect upon and analyze what has taken place.

Types of Documentation

Documentation can be divided into many categories. You can document processes such as the development of self-identity over several years or lunchtime conversations related to a particular topic. The daily agenda collected over time can document the life of the group, or you can ask students the same question on their birthdays and then organize these words together. I see documentation as a series of categories that often overlap. What follows are four categories that have extended my under-standing of documentation and should serve as the beginning of a list that will help you structure your own documentation. I have taken these examples directly from my experience in Reggio Emilia.

- Everyday Life
- Products of *Progettazione*
- Works in Progress
- *Intento Progettuale*

EVERYDAY LIFE

This category involves things that happen in a regular manner at school. This would include the lunchtime example used earlier.

- *Diario:* Notes from each day of the class.
- *Modi di dire:* A collection of funny comments/dialogues from the students over the course of the year.

- *Compleanni:* Birthdays. This book might represent how children answered the same questions on their birthdays, or what they said about their life so far, for example.
- Daily agenda.

PRODUCTS OF *PROGETTAZIONE*

These projects have emerged from the discussions and interests of students and teachers. They may have extended over days, weeks, or months but were individual entities, not tied to the *intento progettuale.*

- *Angeli:* Students' exploration of angels, including words and drawings.
- *Neruda Park:* Students' graphic representations of their school.
- *Smell of fire:* Students' visual representation of their interpretation of the smell of fire.

WORKS IN PROGRESS

These small forms of documentation have emerged from events that occurred in class or in students' lives at home. I found them to be rich and relatively informal in terms of format and presentation. These examples have served the teachers' development greatly in the ways they look at and interpret their students.

- *Conflitti:* A reflection on students' ideas about conflict and its resolution over time.
- Looking towards elementary school

INTENTO PROGETTUALE

These types of documentation are tied directly to the *intento progettuale* and may evolve over one or three years.

- *Dare e darsi identità:* Giving oneself and others identity
- *Segnalibro:* Bookmark
- *Colore tra le mani:* Color among the hands
- *Grafica:* Graphics

In Reggio, students do not regularly take work home but instead keep the majority of their work at school as part of its evolution. The students engage in reflection and selection of pieces to be included in their final body of work, which is presented to their parents at the end of the third year. Thus, the *grafica* is a vast collection of student drawings over three years. The evolution from beginning to end in terms of student development is visible in a collection of this sort. There is no hard and fast rule, but from my observations the documentation tied to the *intento progettuale* went home after three years, while other projects that may have lasted a shorter duration might have been packaged for parents at Christmas or the end of the year.

Great value is placed on keeping student work at school, as this is their place of work and it needs to be available for teachers and students to refer to over time. What goes home and when has been a topic of great discussion among child care professionals working in Reggio-inspired ways. We must keep in mind that in the United States parents are more accustomed to receiving student work regularly. This is something to evaluate and negotiate with the families whose children attend your school in order to strike a balance. You may want to consider having two or three set times a year when students will take home a collection of work. This could be useful to you organizationally as well: you will then have a built-in deadline for revisiting and reflecting on student work. You will still want to send many things home, as they cannot all become part of a finished product. Consider establishing December, March, and June as times to organize and sort student work.

The students will benefit from being involved in this process as well, depending on their age. Developing the student's critical eye can begin at this age. It is interesting and informative to find out what creations they feel particularly good about and why. This is another way to document student development, which brings us full circle to possible types of documentation. By sorting through their drawings with the students, you can take notes on the stories that emerge and the children's own sense of the importance of what they have created. This could become a meta-cognitive portfolio, which uses the graphics as a vehicle to explore the intellectual development of children. The possibilities are endless.

Here is a list of possible documentation products that could result from documenting children's work. Keep in mind that these are only examples—they do not include every product that documentation can ultimately become.

- Wall panels (with or without narrative)
- Booklets
- Posterboards
- Student work assembled on cards
- Books
- Student portfolios of drawings or paintings
- Paintings or drawings on mat board
- Videos
- CDs of photos or music

Documentation panels are one important avenue but are not used to document everything. There are many creative options that frame the work of documentation.

Looking at Your Program

Think about the ways you are already documenting and interpreting the activities of your students. Ask yourself questions like these to tease out what you are already doing:

- Do you take anecdotal records?
- Are there bulletin boards where photos are displayed?
- Is there a sign-in book with notes to parents and succinct commentary on events that occur at school?

All these types of documentation serve different purposes. There may be elements missing from some but included in others. In your notebook, write examples of what is already taking place at your school:

- Do you have a notebook to write notes to yourself?
- What are your colleagues doing to communicate to families?
- How are experiences captured currently? Video? Photo? Audio?
- How is student work collected? Is it re-visited?

By collecting a list of what is already occurring at your school, you will be able to further develop your skills and existing structures instead of beginning anew.

Methods of Documenting

It has been challenging to strike the appropriate balance between the guidance this book is designed to give and creating a checklist that could never truly render the work done in Reggio Emilia. I therefore have created a visual of what could possibly be documented and what might occur in terms of collecting artifacts as the process occurs.

The best way to demonstrate the path of documentation is to share, using the organization of the chart below, a few examples of projects and the accompanying documentation that took place to create a concrete image of the process. The examples discussed below are individual examples that occurred organically, and each could have taken a different path depending on the way the process evolved and the choices made by the teachers and students within the project. There are multiple possibilities that did not occur but could have—the documentation that took place is only one of many potential options.

AS A PROJECT UNFOLDS, YOU MAY BE ...	THE DOCUMENTATION OCCURRING SIMULTANEOUSLY MAY INVOLVE ...
Birth Talking, brainstorming, ping-pong questioning, listening to students	**Birth** Tape-recording conversations, presenting stimulating images, observing behavior and responses and taking notes on what occurs, listening carefully to student contributions, hypotheses
Development Relaunching earlier conversations, synthesizing student comments, reading transcribed conversations, rephrasing questions, defining parameters, taking walking tours, collecting information by consulting families, students, and other adults, visiting relevant and suggestive places	**Development** Tape-recording conversations, presenting stimulating images, observing behavior and responses and taking notes on what occurs, listening carefully to student contributions and hypotheses
Execution Painting, drawing, building with brick, wood, working with wire, working with clay, assembling different materials	**Execution** Taking photos, video taping, tape-recording students as they engage materials, observing students

SEGNALIBRO

When the school year began, Paola and Patty re-visited a question from the year before, and asked the students if four-year-old children read. The students believed that they most definitely could read. As this conversation took place during the morning assembly, Paola managed the discussion while Patty took notes on what the students said. This was the beginning of their documentation, and it was also a habit I noticed. Paola and Patty took a notepad and pencil to the assembly regularly. One would ask the kids questions and manage the group, while the other would take notes, observe the children's actions, and record their words. Sometimes they would use a tape recorder, and both teachers would be involved in the conversation. The tape recorder freed the teachers up to really listen and fully engage the students in the discussion.

The students were asked what they could read, and they shared an interesting list of everyday brands and signs that they could "read." The conversation stopped there, and later that week the teachers reviewed the notes and decided to make a proposal to their students. They invited the children to bring their favorite book to school and read it to their classmates. So the students began to bring books to school to read. Michele was one of the first, and he read a story he knew well. He followed the pictures and words accurately page by page, as the students watched and Paola videotaped his reading. This was another way the teachers chose to gather evidence of the process. The teachers found it interesting that the students believed they could read. One of their questions was, What then was the difference between storytelling and reading? Was it all part of the same activity, a progression towards literacy? When Michele finished reading his book, Paola asked him about his choice of this particular book. Michele responded, "When I read it I hear my mama's words. . . ." Patty took note of this and wrote it down.

Many students continued to bring in books and read to the class, getting videotaped individually. Paola and Patty began to examine and reflect on the artifacts they had collected so far in preparation for an approaching parent meeting: observations, notes from class discussions, and a number of videos of students reading. They began to make informal interpretations about the students' concepts of print and their ability to use picture cues and voice inflection to tell the story. They asked themselves what role these elements played in the children's learning to read.

At the parent meeting Paola and Patty had prepared a presentation for the families on the students' budding literacy. The students' own words were read and video snippets were played for the families. This was the first phase of interpretation. The parents shared information about their children's interest in literature and anecdotes from their home lives that further illuminated the subject. Patty took notes here, too, to include as part of the documentation. These notes were read and discussed in the days following. From them arose the idea of turning down the lights or otherwise modifying the environment while reading a story. Paola asked the children, "Does this change the story?"

This was explored in a variety of ways through the course of the year, with the students' being offered a number of ways to participate. The offerings emerged directly from the documentation collected and the subsequent teacher reflection. Paola then began to synthesize the process in a written booklet, not a final product but a record of the process so far.

In reading about this project, you can see that the documentation was constant and varied and was used to inform the teachers' practice and the direction of the work students engaged in. The teachers could have eventually edited a video of many students together or created a book with photos and observations. This depended on what emerged from the process and what would best illuminate the work and understandings of the children and adults.

FOUR-YEAR-OLDS' PAINTING PROJECT

The painting the four-year-olds created as they contemplated moving upstairs to the five-year-old room was my first independent effort at engaging students and beginning to document the process (see chapter 4 for a full description of this project). The painting project began with a proposal in the assembly by Paola and Patty regarding inhabiting the new space that would be theirs the following year. When the topic was introduced, the tape recorder was used to record the conversation. Patty transcribed the tape that afternoon while the students slept. We looked at what the students had said and decided to take them to visit the space that we were discussing. I took photos of the group as we visited the tower for inspiration. At the early stages we already had transcribed words of children and photos of the students and the space.

When the class had decided on the painting and the subject matter for it, we began the process of creating the artwork. While the students worked, the tape recorder was on, and I took photos of the process. I listened to the tape the first day, but we elected to erase it because it was everyday conversation. The next day I taped the conversation again, and the students had interesting things to say while they worked about how each other painted and the work that had been done the day before. Even though this was not related to what had framed the project (the move to the new space), I transcribed the tape, and Paola, Patty, and I read it over. The project was also a vehicle to look at students' use of color and process of relationships (part of the *intento progettuale*). Since this conversation was related to those projects, we kept the transcript with the photos and other documents to examine later in the process.

I continued photographing and tape-recording the students, using student comments to formulate pointed questions for the students as they worked. The process of documenting the student process was informing my practice as it happened. When the painting was finished, I looked at what I had collected and used this to document my own process as a practitioner. The other avenues for questioning and exploration were numerous, but at the time my growth and development as a teacher were the most obvious choice of a focus for me.

Tools for Documentation

The tools used to gather documentation depend on resources available but can include:

- Tape recorders
- Paper and pen or a laptop for taking notes
- Digital, 35 mm, disposable, or Polaroid camera
- Video camera
- Computer recording software

Components of documentation produced by using these tools:

- Digital or print photos
- Transcripts of student discussions
- Transcripts of adult conversations
- Notes of student or adult conversations
- Videotapes of students working

- Examples of student work
- Student writing
- Student musical compositions
- Observations made while students are working
- Teacher drawings of students' work

In an ideal world every school would be equipped with digital cameras and the latest computer and video technology. Unfortunately this is not often the case. I have found that a digital camera that stores images on a disk inserted in the camera works well for my purposes. I can simply replace the disk and change what I am documenting or give the camera to a colleague to use without having concerns about storage capacity. In Reggio, we used a digital camera that was connected to the computer to download images as well as a 35 mm camera. The latter prevented us from seeing out photos immediately, but the quality of the photos was much better. I have suggested disposable cameras to those without digital or 35 mm cameras. It all serves the same purpose. At a minimum, it is important to have a way of taking photos and a tape recorder. The note-taking and observation require only paper and pencil. A video camera is useful, if available. But these implements are not pivotal in the ability to document. They are certainly helpful but not necessary. It is amazing what a small amount of funding can creatively provide.

Using Documentation

I recall one day at Pablo Neruda when Mara and Patty invited me to join them in the conference room off the entryway in order to plan a panel they wanted to construct. The project involved "the shape of things" in which children examined shapes that surrounded them in nature (circularity, symmetry found in flowers, shells, etc.). We sat down and looked at all of the artifacts on the table, and they discussed what had already been collected while drawing out possibilities and arranging in front of us, like pieces to a puzzle, the various artifacts collected that could create a documentation panel. In front of us were photos, transcriptions of tapes, and samples of student work (drawings and watercolors). We sat for more than an hour sketching possible panels, moving pieces of student work around the table, and trying to create a panel that would represent the teachers' interpretation of the process and the significant events that had occurred. More than one option revealed itself. We left it alone and met again a few days later.

When we met again, Mara, the *atelierista*, had sketched out a synthesis of our discussion, and Patty was able to revisit the discussion. Neither Mara nor Patty had an agenda for what they wanted to document but looked at the materials and talked about what had occurred. Patty shared what had most surprised her as the work took place, and then Mara began sorting through the materials and pulling out pieces that spoke to Patty's comments. They looked at how the project had begun and how it had taken on its own life. The project had revealed the students' inherent understanding of patterns and their ability to identify and replicate patterns found in nature and their surroundings. Students had begun noticing and pointing out patterns of symmetry on their own in moments far from the work done in class. The teachers re-read the students' words captured in tape transcriptions and slowly began to arrange the materials in response to their interpretations. Some things were put aside, and the artifacts that supported their interpretation remained.

In the meantime a large piece of plywood was bolted to the wall and painted a salmon color in anticipation of the panel of documentation that was being constructed. Patty began to post materials on the board as if it were a rough draft. We would walk by, look it over, and discuss it in an effort to work through what might work best for the project we were creating a panel for. The fact that children had started to point out symmetry in other parts of their lives was intriguing to the adults involved and served as a central point around which they were able to organize the process, the languages and products created by the students, and the connections made by students on their own to create a panel that represented the significant lessons of the project. The entire process of creating the panel was as thoughtful as the process of the project itself, and in the end it took several weeks to create the panel.

Creating Documentation Panels in the United States

Once you have started collecting information, how can you use it to interpret and make visible what emerges? Ask yourself questions like these to guide the process of putting the panel together:

- What did you experience while engaging in *progettazione* with your students?
- What surprised you?
- What did you expect to see? What did you actually see?
- Did your students bring in additional experiences or make unexpected connections?

Once during an American workshop, when we had broken up into groups to work on our projects and document the process, one small group followed the progress of another group and documented it. As the second group was negotiating about their panel and how to organize and arrange the documentation, one of the five members at the table simply began using the materials and creating what she considered to be the appropriate documentation without consulting the rest of the group. The first group followed, observed, and photographed the breakdown of the group mentioned. They then created a panel of documentation about the breakdown of the group process that they had witnessed. It was refreshing and clever. They were documenting more than the journey from point A to point B. They were documenting the process of human interactions and group dynamics, which proved to be fertile ground for our exploration of documentation and their own understanding of the possibilities inherent in the process. All of this is just to say: Don't be afraid to ask big questions or get off track. Everything, even or perhaps especially the inevitable breakdowns of the process, is fertile ground for new understandings. In many American programs teaching in this way is breaking new ground. Discomfort, misunderstanding, and cognitive dissonance are essential parts of the process. Treat them with inquiry, as you would treat anything that happened with children, and your understanding will grow.

Using your notebooks, take a few moments to look at a piece of documentation from your program or another, and respond to the questions below. (If you are unable to locate a piece of documentation from a local program, you might use one of the many books published by Reggio Children, which contain much documentation of children's work.)

- What seems to be documented?
- How did you arrive at that conclusion?
- Make a list of concrete components of the documentation you are looking at that support what you are seeing.

- What else might have been documented if the teachers had chosen to do so?
- Are you able to see other pathways the *progettazione* might have taken from what is presented in the documentation?
- How do you think the artifacts were collected?
- Is there evidence of observation? Student work? Questioning and hypothesizing?
- Who would this documentation be useful for? Teachers? Students? Families? Student teachers?

This example of documentation done in the United States brings up many questions, but perhaps the most pressing question heard in all of the workshops hosted around the country was how long it takes until a school can really be working in these Reggio-inspired ways. There is no answer to this question. The time involved for programmatic changes to take root will vary from setting to setting. Remember that in Reggio Emilia they have been working in these ways since after World War II. You must give yourself time and be realistic—any worthwhile change is slow.

When I was working at Pablo Neruda, Mara told me about an archive of documentation in the school. Considering that the school had been open for nearly thirty years, I really wanted to look over the archive! When I did, I saw examples of documentation that resemble things I have seen at schools I have visited in the United States. Seeing the archive brought home to me the truth that the programs that existing in Reggio arrived where they are over time. At the beginning, the programs struggled with many of the same issues that programs in the United States are struggling with now. The documentation they put together in the 1970s did not have the sophistication and depth we are accustomed to seeing in Reggio documentation now.

In the archive, I found samples documenting a project about leaves. Perhaps the most remarkable element was the documentation of the many languages used to explore the topic. There is sight, investigation, graphic, kinesthetic, sculpture, plastic, and painting, each documented on a sheet of pink posterboard. There is clearly a difference between this work and the documentation that is seen from the schools of Reggio today. That is part of the beauty of viewing these old panels— the recognition that the Italians followed a path too.

Refining Your Documentation over Time

When I was able to access the documentation that had been archived at Pablo Neruda, I began to understand the evolution of both the process and the product of documentation in that school. And this is only part of the evolution that the entire process took in Reggio Emilia from the end of World War II until the present day. This should be encouraging to American teachers who are just beginning the process of documenting children's work. Our goal is not to produce documentation that looks like that in the Reggio schools today. Our goal is to document the work of our students and our own work as professionals in a way that reflects the process of learning in our schools as authentically and thoughtfully as possible.

Look at the list you made about the documentation you are already doing at your school. Choose one of the items, and think of it as a vehicle for professional development. How might you use this documentation process that you are already engaged in to look at children's social or emotional development? Here are a couple of examples:

- Could you use the daily agenda to take notes about student behaviors? For example, was it a sunny day and your students particularly energetic? Do you notice a difference in student behavior based on the weather?
- Do parents make comments or ask questions about posted photos? Could you leave a notepad under a bulletin board to serve as an interactive journal with parents or a place to collect their questions and comments on the photos?

These are just a few examples of ways to use what is already in place and extend your practice just a little. The notebook by the bulletin board may serve as a vehicle to build stronger relationships with families. This is exciting for teachers, students, and parents and could evolve into a collection of words from parents accompanied by the photos, telling a story over time.

Documentation can begin simply and on seemingly small topics. It has a tendency to grow quickly, requiring you to look at what is being collected and reflect on it regularly to drive your practice and your own professional development.

Observation Tool for Multiple Children

Date:	**Context:**	**Children:**

Time	Name _____	Name _____

We need to cultivate . . . an atmosphere of reciprocal help and socialization. Implicit in this is a decisive response to a child's need to feel whole. Feeling whole is a biological and cultural necessity for the child (and also for the adult). It is a vital state of well-being.

—LORIS MALAGUZZI

Chapter 6

Families

A fundamental component to the success of any school is the presence of the families whose children go there. Families, including but not limited to parents, are a resource for schools, not a drain on them. Of course they ask questions and make requests, but they do so in the best interests of their children, and the children are the work of a school. For this reason, the families are also the work of the school. As a parent from Reggio shared, "Participating in the school life is very important for a parent, to find out more about the environment in which the children spend so many hours every day, and it is so important for their development." This concept, succinctly stated, is supported through research on the development of children. This research, conducted over the last two decades, has demonstrated that children whose parents are involved are more likely than others to have positive educational outcomes, such as improved academic performance, better school attendance, higher aspirations, reduced dropout rates, and increased graduation rates.

Since the role of the family is vital to the success of a child and a school, it is critical to think about how families are involved in our programs. In this chapter we will start by reflecting on your own school experience and the role your family played. Then we will discuss the role of families in the schools of Reggio Emilia. This will include how families are brought "inside the story" of their children and their schools. From there you will look carefully at the value you place on family participation in both positive and negative terms. This will be based on your experiences as a child and as an educator, and your vision of what a school for young children includes. Then these will be woven together to create a framework for family participation that is aligned with your school vision. This will provide the opportunity to look at your own work and the work of other schools in an effort to begin developing a plan that "fits" your school reality.

Revisiting Your Values: What Is the Role of Families in Education?

Think about your own experience as a child as far back as you can remember through high school. Write in a detailed manner as possible the memories you have of your family going to your school. This should include "back to school" nights, parent–teacher conferences, open houses, school plays, Christmas performances, graduations, father–daughter picnics, car washes, dances your parents chaperoned, football games, track meets—any time your family came to an event that occurred at school.

When you have written about these memories, make a list of ten adjectives to describe the feelings you have associated with these memories. Once you have done this, describe the memories that came to mind first—perhaps the first day of kindergarten when your mother stayed half of the day, or when your family was in the fifth row at the holiday performance taking photos and applauding. Focus on the feelings that still emerge when you think about these experiences.

Next, consider your values about families in education from your current professional position. Look back at what you wrote in chapter 1, and then answer these questions again, thinking in particular about the relationship of the child to her or his family:

- Who is a child?
- What is childhood?
- How do we learn?
- How do children learn?
- What is the meaning of *to educate*?
- What is the role of school in society?
- What is the role of families in the education of children?

These questions will contribute to your definition of family participation and your vision of where it fits into your school. If you view childhood as a time of freedom with strong family connections, this will help shape your approach to participation. If you believe that children construct knowledge, then you must think about what their families have to do with the knowledge they construct and how the knowledge they construct at home and at school interacts. Go through your responses to the questions above and try to extend your responses, linking them to the participation of families in your educational project.

Values about Parents in Reggio

In Reggio Emilia the role that families play in the preschools deserves particular attention. Family participation is seen as essential to both the families and to the school. In Reggio there were innumerable ways for parents to be engaged in the school experience. A few examples include: work evenings to prepare for events or help the teachers prepare materials, class meetings, holiday parties, and meetings around issues that involved families, such as the birth of new siblings or the nutrition of small children. There were also larger initiatives offered at a community level to examine specific topics or to present speakers such as Dr. Jerome Bruner or Daniel Goleman in a public forum for any community members interested.

Other opportunities included time at the school, which was open early and late enough for parents to come and play with their children both before and after school. Sometimes there were performances that parents would prepare, such as plays and puppet shows for events including graduation or Christmas. In preparation for the annual *consegno* or "consignment" in English (an afternoon when the students leaving the school would celebrate and present their parents with the body of work they had created over three years), there were paintings to be matted, collections of student drawings to be organized in the individual folders, and other tasks to put the finishing touches on each student's work. Parents of the younger students did this for the parents of the five-year-olds as a gracious gesture.

A school party might need *cappelletti,* a traditional filled pasta made by hand. This meant an evening of mothers, grandmothers, aunts, and friends working together while visiting and accomplishing the task, making homemade pasta for the school community. The women were delighted with the American among them, with one grandmother having me sit next to her so she could assist me and supervise the pasta I was making. It was a fun and lighthearted evening passed in company, which ultimately served the school by preparing something the teachers needed. Those offerings are collected and encouraged through a web of opportunities but in a manner that is totally natural. To go and spend time at the school and to have parents constantly present for many reasons are seen as a part of the work of a school.

My first parents' meeting at Pablo Neruda took place at the beginning of the school year, when the four-year-olds were returning for their second year. The evening meeting's theme was continuity and change. The teachers, Paola and Patty, proceeded to share an image of the class as a group, a composite, without getting into the specifics of individual children. They shared the projects they had carried over from the previous year as well as what they intended to explore this year as stated in the *intento progettuale.* The parents listened intently and absorbed what was offered about the children as a group without asking questions about individual children until the end, when the meeting broke up and they were able to approach the teachers individually. It struck me as an incredibly civilized meeting, as parents listened and explored the intellectual, social, emotional, and physical development of their children as a group. The meeting passed rather quickly without a great deal of jargon.

I was also invited to the same meeting for the five-year-old class, taught by Antonia and Lara. This meeting followed much of the same format, while having a different flavor due to the individual parents and teachers present. I remember being surprised at the high level yet relaxed communication between the parents and teachers regarding cognition and development without veering to the subject of individual children. It was refreshing to see parents identify their children as members of a group instead of only as individuals with individual needs. Here, at least on these evenings, the children were represented as a group in which they each took part and played a role. All of the schools had class meetings. Other kinds of regular family participation existed at all schools, determined by the teachers and needs of the school.

On one occasion, Paola and Patty organized a work evening, in which parents came to prepare materials for the message project. At Pablo Neruda the students each had their own mailbox, and, beginning at three years old, they created and exchanged messages with their classmates. An important element of the project are the materials: letters, photos, ribbon, magazine pictures, and each student's first and last name printed from the computer. These materials were cut and organized so they were inviting and readily available for children to use in creating messages that they could exchange with one another. The parents came for a couple of hours to cut and chat and organize. The next day, when the children came to school, they were visibly proud of the materials that had been prepared. The children knew their parents had come the previous evening to do this work for them. "Julie, my mom came last night and made these . . . ," said Laura, as she held up postage-stamp–sized photos of each child that had been carefully photocopied and cut and filed individually and alphabetically according to the name of the child.

Participation at the *nido* has a different look and purpose. The work done there supports parents exploring topics of interest that relate to young children while facilitating the building of relationships among families. The families can serve as resources to one another with their varying degrees of parenting experience and can offer support and humor to other parents. The *nido* also paves the way for the introduction of new things, such as beginning new foods, understanding children's behavior, and toilet training. The opportunities offered to parents at a *nido* focus on parenting in addition to the traditional parties and projects one might find at the *scuola dell'infanzia*. These differences between the *nidi* and preschools are driven by the needs of the families. The *nido* invites the parents to get to know each other and serves as a resource in many ways. The *nido* also connects parents so they can be supports for one another, having children of the same age and developmental point. One of the parents I came to know as a friend in Reggio, whose children attended Nido Rodari and the Diana School, Margherita Sani, spoke of feeling as though she had a community to consult and share with as a parent, thanks to the school that built a community through the participation opportunities that brought families together.

The following schedule of parent meetings was offered to parents in the spring of 2000 at Nido Bellelli. The topics were determined based on the informal discussions teachers had with parents at pick up and drop off. The meetings were both lively and well attended.

Tuesday, March 28
Do families who have children need to think about, construct, and respect new rules?

Tuesday, April 4
What motivation was involved in the choice to have one or more children? Do children bring a wealth or a limit to families?

Monday, April 17
Mothers and fathers in their relationship with children today: What changes have occurred in the role of the father and the mother?

American schools can take much away from the Reggio schools' habits of involving parents. There are tangible and intangible benefits for everyone involved: children, families, and teachers. School is the central point in the lives of children, and when families share in the school, children's pride and sense of connection is palpable. When families are "inside the story" of school, then parents, grandparents, and siblings are provided the opportunity to know children in an entirely new way. Children can show parts of themselves as they are with peers, other adults, authority figures, and materials, for instance. Growth that may otherwise not present itself in the daily life lived by a family may be clearly visible in another context in which the child is comfortable— school. This also gives children the opportunity to share who they are becoming with their families, things they are proud of and have acquired as they are developing.

Being welcomed and included in the school experience offers families an opportunity to know one another in new ways that are playful, celebratory, and fun. Margherita Sani, whose children attended the Diana School, was once invited to participate in a Christmas production at Diana when her son Giovanni was there. Margherita arrived for what she thought was an evening of organizing a production the children would perform, only to find that it was to be a play performed by the parents for the children! She was surprised, but stayed to work with other parents on this performance, in which each parent took the role of an animal. Margherita spoke fondly of the experience. She said it was a challenge to go several evenings a week for a brief period of time but at the same time found it engaging to "play" with other adults while preparing something for their children. When the performance was given, she said it was quite fun and that the children were delighted by it. Margherita wrote, "The schools have offered me the occasions to grow as a person, to widen my horizons, but also, by involving me in playful activities with my own children, as well as with other kids, to rediscover and bring out the child in me."

Through their presence at their children's preschool, parents can become well informed about their child's development and development in general. For example, spending time in school offers the possibility of watching a child with others of the same age and noticing how he fits with his age group regarding:

- interest in teaming
- social skills and ability to work in a group
- self-reliance
- interest and excitement about school

Families also have the opportunity to work with other families who share a common experience and the philosophy of involvement with their children. The presence of parents gives teachers and parents the chance to build a relationship and create a regular exchange of advice and information about the children.

In addition, through discussions with parents, teachers expand their ideas about the children's work, development, and personalities. They get tangible help with tasks that need to be accomplished and the experience of being part of a larger community of families. This just touches on the potential value of regular participation on the part of families. The bottom line is that the regular participation of families is what is best for children, and every educational project is about the children.

Looking at Your Program: Parent Participation

It is important to first take a look at where you are as a school and community. There are so many ways to have families participate in schools. Think carefully about what the ideal parent presence would be in your ideal school. Take some time to write about the following:

- Define family participation in your own words.
- How are parents currently participating in your school?
- What are the possible ways families can participate?
- How would you like your families to be participating?
- What would be the benefits of having families take a larger interest in the development of their children rather than asking what they ate and whether or not they slept?
- What would it be like to have parents meeting as groups?
- How might parents support the school in ways that are not only economic?
- What would the parents have to offer?
- When would this occur?
- How would the school invite the parents to become involved?
- How would parents connect with their children through this participation?
- How would the parent–child–teacher triad be cultivated and sustained?
- What would the first steps be?
- What would motivate even busy or single parents to engage?

Your thoughtful responses to the queries above will be pivotal in shaping the participation component of your school as this chapter progresses.

Parent Participation in Reggio Emilia

Family is truly the basis of the Italian culture. The sense of belonging and connection is very strong, and familial ties are important. Families are close, and children are held close well into adulthood. It is not uncommon for singles well into their thirties to still live at home with the family, the mother still caring for her children by cooking meals, doing laundry, and ironing, for instance. There is not a large group of adult singles living independently. When it is time to go to college, a large majority of Italians live at home rather than moving away and living in the dorms or apartments, as is more common in the United States. Thus the regular involvement of family members in each other's lives is the norm. Families are valued by one another and in the society as a whole. There is no big push for children to be on their own or go out into the world and make their way.

This strong component of the culture is equally present in the schools for young children. It is not so much that there is a different value placed on family participation in Italian schools; it is just a more implicit part of life. In the United States many families are headed by single parents or two parents who both work outside the home. It is also important to remember that Americans have a different relationship with time. It seems that we have much less of it or that our days are more hurried than when I lived in Italy. Americans work many hours, while the Italians keep a more reasonable schedule of thirty-five to forty hours a week. These are all important factors to keep in mind when thinking about why the level of participation in Reggio is so exceptional. Barriers exist for Americans that are not commonly found in Italy.

The parents of Reggio Emilia also participate because the *reggiani* have developed offerings that are engaging and playful. Parents would participate regardless, but it is fun for them as well. The schools of Reggio do this very well: they offer unusual events that appeal to both adults and children. Here are some of the experiences involving families that I was able to observe while working in Reggio. This is by no means a complete list, as there are endless ways to include families in schools. Treat this as a beginning that can help you generate ideas. I have divided the types of participation opportunities into three categories:

1. Habitual Opportunities

- Class meetings (three times a year)
- Holiday parties
- End-of-year party *(consegno)*
- Parent discussion evenings: These occur at the *nido* revolving around topics of interest to parents of babies and toddlers.
- Drop off/pick up: An opportunity to visit with other families and play with children in the yard or classroom.
- Writing seminars: Nido Rodari offers a few evenings of examining Rodari's work, and parents are able to explore his writing and do some of their own.
- Contributing to the writing and publication of a school newspaper.
- Building implements for class: parents build light tables, construction platforms, and mirror triangles.

2. Work Evenings

- Cooking
- Material preparation for classes
- Decorating and preparation for events
- Creation of art and books: Nido Rodari invites parents and older children to create books for the newest students representing elements of their lives. The materials are available before and after school for families to work on the project when they have time.

3. Special Events

- Plays
- Musicals
- Dances
- Fundraisers: A sort of tag sale is held in a square in Reggio, and children bring objects from home to sell; families attend and assist with the sale.
- Community initiatives: events offered by the Comune di Reggio Emilia— for example, a Saturday when the recycling center is open for families to make crafts.

Creating Change in Your Program: Getting Families inside the Story

Margherita Sani told me something else that struck me about her experience as a parent in the schools of Reggio:

> Class meetings, conferences, and other events the school organizes offered me a chance to reflect on how I was behaving as a parent, to compare views with other parents and with the educators, also a chance to deal with more wide-ranging issues, which have an impact on the daily life with children. Likewise, it is important for the school to encourage parents' participation, to receive both practical and intellectual support on many matters, but also to know how society, lifestyles, family patterns really are and change.

When I think about family participation in Reggio, I have a visual image of a web of activities that seem to "catch" the families and offer them so many opportunities that are both enticing and joyful—it is virtually impossible to refuse them all. You can create a similar web in your program. Think first about those adjectives: *enticing* and *joyful.* Bring them back to your mind again and again as you think about making more room for parents in your program.

In order to create a web of participation opportunities, take a look at what you wrote about how your families are currently participating and how you would like to see them participating. Using these ideas as the foundation, coupled with the thoughts of Margherita and the examples she speaks of, let us take a moment to begin creating a web of participation opportunities that will both support and engage your parents.

Here are some suggestions to help you create your web, which will grow over time:

- Offer participation opportunities at different times—before school, during school, after school, on weekends. Perhaps some parents can come and help set up for lunch and dine with the students once a week.
- To accommodate varying work and family schedules, parent meetings may need to occur more than once. Schedule one in the evening or on the weekend.
- If you are having a work evening, put out work that parents can do at drop off or pick up; these may be more relaxed times for some parents.

- Invite parents personally to events rather than just sending a flyer home or posting the invitation on a bulletin board. While a general announcement can help make sure that all families have heard about the event, a flyer cannot replace a personal invitation.
- Always offer refreshments, even if they are simple ones. Events seem to take on a social dimension when refreshments are available. Even work meetings can become fun when there are food and drink to enjoy. Food is a big socializing agent in Italy, and it is very much the norm to serve bottled water, cakes, cookies, or fruit. This creates a more relaxed, friendly experience.
- Offer the opportunity for parents to work at home to contribute something concrete to the program. Parents may be able to build, write, design, or paint things that are useful and contribute to the children's educational experience. This is a daily reminder of the family member's presence for the child.
- Be sure to offer interpreting services (American Sign Language or other languages relevant to your families) and celebrate and embrace all cultures in the school's community. This may mean a general group event that includes everyone with appropriate language interpreting; a meeting that is held in several sessions, each in a different language; or celebrations of a specific culture, such as the Day of the Dead if there are Latino students or a Chinese New Year parade for the Chinese families. All families will enjoy the celebrations, and it will build community across the diverse cultures. Thanksgiving may be traditional for some, while others choose to honor Native American heritage. Be cautious about holiday celebrations, and solicit input from the families and teachers.

Make a list in your journal of several options for each of the three categories of parent involvement: Habitual, Work Evenings, and Special Events. Choose ideas that reflect your understanding about children and families and your view of education in the life of young children, and ideas that seem possible within the framework of your program. Think in terms of baby steps: How can you expand on what you are already doing? How can you open one door?

When you have your list, pick one or two as your foundation. Then talk to your families, and find out what interests them and what timing would be best for them. Remember those key words: *enticing* and *joyful*. What will be enticing and joyful for the families in your center? It is important to have input from as many people as possible, but don't be overwhelmed by all the feedback you get. Begin with a few fixed events, and continue adding opportunities over time. Some of these will work well and become part of your program, while others will not fit, and you will abandon them. Like all the other big changes you will make as you begin to work in Reggio-like ways, the participation piece of your program must evolve over time. Remember the fifty-year history of the Reggio programs. Look at other schools, talk to colleagues, find out what elementary schools in your area do, and adapt these ideas to your setting. You may not get all of the participation you want right away, but over time, as layer upon layer is added and the school reputation becomes one of active participation, the school will attract those who value participation.

Once you have created your list under each category and chosen the events you will begin with, continue writing about and reflecting on these events as they occur. Be sure to notice who attends, whether or not they arrive on time, and when they leave. It is easy to remember something fondly in retrospect that actually was not that great. As soon as possible following a meeting or celebration, write down your observations of the parents. This is another place to put your observation and inquiry skills into practice. Document the event by asking yourself questions like these:

- How engaged were the participants? When were they most engaged? How do you know?
- What interesting questions were raised by the event? What do you want to investigate further?
- How will the event affect the daily life of the school or the classroom?
- Was the goal of the event achieved in an enjoyable manner? If the goal of the evening was to prepare materials for the classroom, did you get what was needed? If you planned a class meeting to discuss early literacy, did parents talk and share the routines they have with their children?
- What did it feel like? Was it formal or lighthearted?

By documenting the experience, you will be able to refine what you offer families and how you offer it so that you successfully get parents "inside the story."

However you plan your family participation, be sure that it is feeding your declared values about children and education. For example, I like to think of school as fun, a place that I want to be. I would like for parents of children in the school to see it in a similar manner. The school can be an escape: it can offer parents a respite from both home and work where they can spend a bit of quality, unhurried time with their child. I once heard a teacher talk about the number of hours parents were required to contribute annually. Do we really want parents to see participating in their children's school as an obligation? (Remember those words—*enticing* and *joyful*.) In one case a school discussed making a certain number of hours mandatory for parents to contribute and tracking the hours in a ledger. I have also heard programs discuss offering parents the opportunity to write a check to buy their way out of giving time. I would never discourage financial contributions to schools, but giving money is a passive form of participation. It does not create all the advantages to children, to the school, and to the families themselves that true involvement does. If we view children as competent beings who deserve the support of their families, then we will make it our purpose to create opportunities that are inviting and enjoyable for all families to come to schools.

Malaguzzi, Loris
    on creativity, 48
    on environment, 24
    on "hundred languages," x
    on interpretation, 96
    on *progettazione,* 64, 68
    on views of children, 10,
    17–18
    on wholeness, 122
    and Reggio Emilia origins, 1
mealtimes, 20, 55
mini-atelier, 8
mirrors, 16–17, 29, 43

naps. *See* rest time
nidi, 8, 29–30, 127–128

objectives, 17
observation, 98, 100–106
    scheduling, 104, 106
    tools for, 102–104, 105, 121
outdoor play, 104

parents. *See* family involvement
pedagogista, 8
piazza, 29, 38
pick-up time, 55
private/public space. *See* individ-
    ual/group relationships
progettazione, 66–94
    change process, 91–94
    components of, 83–89
    defined, 8–9, 70–72
    and documentation, 89, 98,
    109–111
    reflective practice, 67–68, 82
    sample project, 89–91
    and views of children, 66–67
    See also progettazione in the
    Reggio approach

progettazione in the Reggio
    approach, 68–82
    daily life projects, 80–81
    defined, 70–72
    environmental projects,
    79–80
    intento progettuale, 71–72,
    74–79
    overview, 68–70, 73
    self-managed projects, 81–82
projects. *See progettazione*
project time, 54–55
provoazione, 9, 38, 42
provocare, 9

questioning strategies, 77–78,
    83–86

reflective practice, 5
    documentation, 111,
    118–119
    environment, 37, 42–43
    examples of, 20–21
    family involvement, 130
    progettazione, 67–68, 82
    in Reggio approach, 32–33
    space, 28–29, 32–33
    time, 51, 60–62
    views of children, 13, 14–15,
    18–21
Reggio approach
    barriers to adopting, 3–5
    change in, 32–33, 40–41,
    43–44
    environment in, 35–36,
    38–42, 43–44
    family involvement in,
    125–130, 131–132
    reflective practice in, 32–33
    space in, 29–33

Other Resources from Redleaf Press

Poking, Pinching and Pretending: Documenting Toddlers' Explorations with Clay
by Dee Smith and Jeanne Goldhaber
Poking, Pinching, and Pretending investigates how one group of infants and toddlers learns about clay as an early "language." Inspired by the programs in Reggio Emilia, this guide encourages educators to share the questions and theories that come from observing and documenting children's interactions with clay to heighten their understanding of how toddlers explore, represent, and learn.

Designs for Living and Learning: Transforming Early Childhood Environments
by Deb Curtis and Margie Carter
Drawing inspiration from a variety of approaches, from Waldorf to Montessori to Reggio to Greenman, Prescott, and Olds, *Designs for Living and Learning* outlines hundreds of ways to create healthy and inviting physical, social, and emotional environments for children in child care.

The Art of Awareness: How Observation Can Transform Your Teaching
by Deb Curtis and Margie Carter
Do more than watch children—with children. Covering different aspects of children's lives and how to observe them, as well as tips for gathering and preparing documentation, *The Art of Awareness* is an inspiring look at how to see the children in your care—and how to see what they see.

Reflecting Children's Lives: A Handbook for Planning Child-Centered Curriculum
by Deb Curtis and Margie Carter
Keep children and childhood at the center of your curriculum and rethink ideas about scheduling, observation, play, materials, space, and emergent themes with these original approaches.

Theories of Childhood: An Introduction to Dewey, Montessori, Erikson, Piaget, and Vygotsky
by Carol Garhart Mooney
Theories of Childhood examines the work of five groundbreaking educational theorists in relation early education. Each theorist's ideas are presented to help teachers and students look to the foundations of child care for solutions and guidance in classrooms today.

Focused Early Learning: A Planning Framework for Teaching Young Children
by Gaye Gronlund
Focused Early Learning provides a simple and innovative framework for organizing teaching plans into a realistic, classroom-based format that focuses on the unique needs of each child.

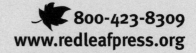 **800-423-8309**
www.redleafpress.org